CONTEMPORARY WRITERS

General Editors
MALCOLM BRADBURY
and
CHRISTOPHER BIGSBY

PATRICK WHITE

IN THE SAME SERIES

Donald Barthelme   *M. Couturier and R. Durand*
Saul Bellow   *Malcolm Bradbury*
Richard Brautigan   *Marc Chénetier*
John Fowles   *Peter Conradi*
Graham Greene   *John Spurling*
Seamus Heaney   *Blake Morrison*
Philip Larkin   *Andrew Motion*
Doris Lessing   *Lorna Sage*
Malcolm Lowry   *Ronald Binns*
Iris Murdoch   *Richard Todd*
Joe Orton   *C. W. E. Bigsby*
Harold Pinter   *G. Almansi and S. Henderson*
Thomas Pynchon   *Tony Tanner*
Alain Robbe-Grillet   *John Fletcher*
Philip Roth   *Hermione Lee*
Kurt Vonnegut   *Jerome Klinkowitz*

PATRICK
WHITE

JOHN COLMER

METHUEN
LONDON AND NEW YORK

First published in 1984 by
Methuen & Co. Ltd
11 New Fetter Lane, London EC4P 4EE
Published in the USA by
Methuen & Co.
in association with Methuen, Inc.
733 Third Avenue, New York, NY 10017

Typeset by Rowland Phototypesetting Ltd
Printed in Great Britain by
Richard Clay (The Chaucer Press) Ltd
Bungay, Suffolk

British Library Cataloguing in Publication Data

Colmer, John
Patrick White. – (Contemporary writers)
1. White, Patrick – Criticism and interpretation
I. Title   II. Series
823   PR9619.3.W5Z/

ISBN 0-416-36790-9

Library of Congress Cataloging in Publication Data

Colmer, John
Patrick White
(Contemporary writers)
Bibliography: p.
1. White, Patrick, 1912 –   – Criticism and interpretation.
I. Title.   II. Series.
PR9619.3.W559   1984   823   84-14676
ISBN 0-416-36790-9 (pbk.)

CONTENTS

General editors' preface   6
Acknowledgements   8
A note on the texts   9

1   Introduction and early fiction   11
2   Middle novels: Australian epics   28
3   Middle novels: artists and visionaries   42
4   Plays and short stories   57
5   Last novels: 'The ordinary ones'   69
6   Conclusion: White and the critics   85

Notes   88
Bibliography   90

GENERAL EDITORS' PREFACE

The contemporary is a country which we all inhabit, but there is little agreement as to its boundaries or its shape. The serious writer is one of its most sensitive interpreters, but criticism is notoriously cautious in offering a response or making a judgement. Accordingly, this continuing series is an endeavour to look at some of the most important writers of our time, and the questions raised by their work. It is, in effect, an attempt to map the contemporary, to describe its aesthetic and moral topography.

The series came into existence out of two convictions. One was that, despite all the modern pressures on the writer and on literary culture, we live in a major creative time, as vigorous and alive in its distinctive way as any that went before. The other was that, though criticism itself tends to grow more theoretical and apparently indifferent to contemporary creation, there are grounds for a lively aesthetic debate. This series, which includes books written from various standpoints, is meant to provide a forum for that debate. By design, some of those who have contributed are themselves writers, willing to respond to their contemporaries; others are critics who have brought to the discussion of current writing the spirit of contemporary criticism or simply a conviction, forcibly and coherently argued, for the contemporary significance of their subjects. Our aim, as the series develops, is to continue to explore the works of major post-war writers – in fiction, drama and poetry – over an international range, and thereby to illuminate not only those works but also in some degree the artistic, social and moral assumptions on which they rest. Our wish is that, in their very variety of approach and emphasis, these books will stimulate interest in and understanding of the vitality of a living literature which, because it is contemporary, is especially ours.

Norwich, England   MALCOLM BRADBURY
                                                 CHRISTOPHER BIGSBY

ACKNOWLEDGEMENTS

In the following pages I have sometimes drawn on my published writings on Patrick White and I am grateful to the respective editors and publishers for permission to use material from the following: *Patrick White: 'Riders in the Chariot'* (Melbourne: Edward Arnold, 1978); 'Duality in Patrick White', in *Patrick White: A Critical Symposium*, ed. R. Shepherd and K. Singh (Adelaide: Flinders University of South Australia, 1978); 'The Quest Motif in Patrick White', *Review of National Literatures*, 11 (1983), pp. 192–210; and 'Patrick White: *A Fringe of Leaves*', *The Literary Half-Yearly*, 23, 2 (July 1982), pp. 85–100.

I wish also to acknowledge the kind permission of Patrick White, his agents Curtis Brown Ltd, and his publishers, Harrap, Jonathan Cape, Viking Press, Penguin Books, Sun Books (Macmillan, Australia) and Currency Press, for permission to quote from his works.

Finally I wish to express my gratitude to the University of Adelaide for granting me study leave, to my wife for her patient help and encouragement, to David Tacey and others for sharing ideas with me, and to Lesley Robinson for typing the manuscript.

London, 1984   JOHN COLMER

A NOTE ON THE TEXTS

Page references to quotations from Patrick White's works are to the recent Penguin editions unless otherwise stated. The following abbreviations have been used and the works are listed in chronological order.

HV   *Happy Valley* (London: Harrap, 1939)
LD   *The Living and the Dead*
AS   *The Aunt's Story*
TM   *The Tree of Man*
V   *Voss*
RC   *Riders in the Chariot*
BO   *The Burnt Ones*
FP   *Four Plays* (Melbourne: Sun Books, 1967)
SM   *The Solid Mandala*
Viv   *The Vivisector*
ES   *The Eye of the Storm*
C   *The Cockatoos*
FL   *A Fringe of Leaves*
BT   *Big Toys* (Sydney: Currency Press, 1978)
TA   *The Twyborn Affair*
FG   *Flaws in the Glass*
SD   *Signal Driver* (Sydney: Currency Press, 1983)
N   *Netherwood* (Sydney: Currency Press, 1983)

1

INTRODUCTION
AND EARLY FICTION

Patrick White is a giant among the moderns. He offers a completely new experience to readers who are mainly familiar with the recent British novel. They will have encountered little that is comparable to his grand, archetypal themes and grotesque modes, except perhaps in the epic scale and metaphysical panorama of painter-novelists like Wyndham Lewis and Mervyn Peake. Patrick White is himself a frustrated painter and musician. He speaks in his autobiographical essay, 'The Prodigal Son', of wishing to produce in his fiction 'the textures of music, the sensuousness of paint . . . what Delacroix and Blake might have seen, what Mahler and Liszt may have heard' (p. 157). From such a novelist we cannot expect the social realism and decent, liberal morality of the British tradition or the formal experimentation and extreme self-consciousness of the post-modernist American novel. His mentors are Dickens, Dostoevsky and Melville. His mammoth fictions possess the amplitude of theme and profusion of detail of the great nineteenth-century novel, combined with stream-of-consciousness techniques associated with James Joyce, Virginia Woolf and William Faulkner. He also owes a general debt to European expressionism, which taught him the value of grotesque and distorted forms for expressing the irrational in human nature. Yet, in spite of such obvious debts, he has created a wholly individual kind of novel. Few modern writers have found more varied ways of dramatizing the dynamic

11

tension between inner and outer worlds or of exploring the quest for meaning in an apparently meaningless universe. He had also created a highly personal style, so that almost any page bears the unmistakable signature of his total world view. His vision is both eclectic and eccentric. It has much in common with the social and moral paradoxes that underlie Blake's poetry, and owes much, as the epigraphs make clear, to pioneer thinkers of the modern tradition, ranging from Mahatma Gandhi to Paul Eluard. His major novels, unlike so much sceptical recent fiction, move inexorably towards some grand, positive affirmation about life.

From the start it is important to recognize White's conflicting loyalties to Europe and Australia. He was born in London in 1912 when his wealthy parents were on an extended honeymoon. They belonged to the Australian class which educated its sons at English public schools and Oxford and Cambridge, spent long periods in Europe, rented English country houses and Mediterranean villas, lived a patrician, privileged life, and owned vast sheep properties the size of a large English county. White's father gave him a generous allowance that set him free to travel widely in Europe and America and to become a writer. He was nearly 40 when he returned to settle in Australia. The land he returned to was very different from the one he had left in the inter-war years. Politically and economically, it was no longer so dependent on the 'home' country; culturally, it was developing vigorous national traditions, especially through the expressionist paintings of Drysdale and Nolan, two artists with whom White shared a revitalized image of the vastness and mystery of the Australian outback. But, to White's horror and dismay, the increased prosperity and independence seemed to exacerbate the materialism, philistinism and tasteless gentility of Australian suburban culture. Europe and Australia, the beauty of the landscape and the philistinism of the suburbs – these are the poles between which White's fiction moves.

White is now internationally famous. Books on his work have been published in Australia, Britain, Canada and Sweden.

Faced with such a formidably difficult writer, critics have naturally concentrated on patient exegesis. They have also paid tribute to his genius – formally recognized by the award of a Nobel Prize in 1973. But there has been little attempt at evaluation and even the most recent critical books appeared before *The Twyborn Affair* (1979) and the autobiography *Flaws in the Glass* (1981), both of which throw new light on his whole career; they also appeared before the publication of his last three plays. My own brief study covers the whole of White's published work and combines a personal evaluation of his achievement with the kind of exegesis that readers coming to some of the works for the first time may find useful.

My account also differs from many others in stressing the duality of White's vision, not its unity, and in regarding him as a secular salvationist, not a religious writer, in spite of his remark to Craig McGregor: 'Religion. Yes, that's behind all my books.' It differs, too, in drawing extensively on the recently published autobiography *Flaws in the Glass* and in directing attention to White's work in the theatre. It not only establishes various links between the plays and the novels but also stresses the dramatic tensions in White between the frustrated actor and the self-conscious revenant, between the artist who lives through others and the solitary gazer into the distorting mirrors of the self. His description of his experience as a 14-year-old in the English neo-Gothic house rented by his parents illustrates the central significance of the mirror image:

> There was the Long Room, at one end the garden, at the other the great gilded mirror, all blotches and dimples and ripples. I fluctuated in the watery glass; according to the light I retreated into the depths of the aquarium, or trembled in the foreground like a thread of pale-green samphire. Those who thought they knew me were ignorant of the creature I scarcely knew myself. (*FG*, p. 1)

In similar fashion almost all his characters gaze into mirrors; for White, progressive revelations of the undiscovered self culminate in *The Twyborn Affair* in the vision of memory as a long hall of mirrors, reflecting and refracting the extreme polarities of human experience (*TA*, p. 351).

*

Patrick White's works are rooted in the painful drama of his early life. 'In the theatre of my imagination I should say there are three or four basic sets, all of them linked to the actual past, which can be dismantled and reconstructed to accommodate the illusion of reality life boils down to' (*FG*, p. 154). Most of the sets combine a symbolic house, distorting mirrors, a wild garden and a privileged visionary whose life has been moulded by an ineffective father and a dominating mother. But because everything he has written has been 'dredged up from the unconscious', the transposition of life into art has been a rich and complex affair. Over and over again, White has insisted that he is not a realistic writer, nor a cerebral one, nor a moralist who 'preaches sermons' in his books. Nevertheless, it is true that his central moral and imaginative preoccupation has been to discover a unity that would transcend the obvious dualities of existence. In his seventies he seems to have become reconciled to a limited achievement both in life and art. 'The ultimate spiritual union is probably as impossible to achieve as the perfect work of art or the unflawed human relationship. In matters of faith, art, and love I have had to reconcile myself to starting again where I began' (*FG*, p. 74).

He began early. He wrote a play, *The Mexican Bandits* (1921), when he was 9 years old, a piece of romantic fiction a few years later, and three novels 'more honest in their lumbering truth than my subsequent chase after a fashionable style in London' (*FG*, p. 52) when he worked for two years, between public school and Cambridge, as a jackeroo undergoing the practical training usual for young men expected later to manage a large property of their own. In his first published short story, 'The Twitching Colonel', printed in the *London Mercury* in June 1937, one of the basic theatrical sets emerges clearly. The story is structured on a contrast between two views of reality and two responses to life; these are developed

14

through the eccentric retired English colonel who remembers a mystical experience in India and his complacent wife who is 'attached to her self beyond escaping'. It is typical of the later fiction that the privileged visionary is placed against a sordid physical environment and a background of jeering, uncomprehending people. Typical too is the narrative trajectory from the present to the past; the colonel's illumination and escape from the self comes from the memory of a visionary moment in the past and is accompanied by personal dissolution in fire. Fires — real and as symbols of purifying intensity and destructive passions — are to recur memorably at the Hotel du Midi in *The Aunt's Story* (1948) and in the Madeleine episode in *The Tree of Man* (1955). The highly lyric style of 'The Twitching Colonel', which incorporates irony and breaks all conventional syntactic rules, also foreshadows White's later daring mixture of modes and his strikingly individual style.

Central to all White's later fiction is the distinction made in the short story between external appearance and internal reality, between surface meaning and underlying significance. Through the creation of this duality he invests his world with spiritual values. For human beings the gap between the inner and outer self is often wide, as the eccentric Miss Hare feels at the beginning of *Riders in the Chariot* (1961).

> Where the road sloped down she ran, disturbing stones, her body quite agitated as it accompanied her, but her inner self by now joyfully serene. The anomaly of that relationship never failed to mystify, and she stopped again, to consider. For a variety of reasons, very little of her secret, actual nature had been disclosed to other human beings. (*RC*, p. 11)

Neither is the natural world always what it seems. A special insight is required to perceive its reality. This, Miss Hare possesses: 'All that land, stick and stone, belonged to her, over and above actual rights. Nobody else had ever known how to penetrate it quite to the same extent (*RC*, p. 12). Only White's visionaries have the power to read nature aright and see into the heart of things.

15

The contrast in 'The Twitching Colonel' between spirituality and complacent materialism has its roots deep in White's early life. His first intimations of another world came through wax effigies, witches and the Mad Woman of Sydney, dangling her 'fish skeletons and heads', who in his boyhood eyes 'took on a significance above daylight and reality' (*FG*, p. 20). As his autobiography reveals, he suffered acutely as a potential artist in a complacent, wealthy environment. 'An artist in the family was almost like a sodomite; if you had one you kept him dark' (*FG*, p. 57) – or tried to transform him into an English gentleman. White received his first 'wounds' at an Australian prep school before satisfying his mother's colonial ambitions by serving his four years' 'prison sentence' at an English public school, Cheltenham.

He found temporary escape from English manners and Australian materialism during his two years as a jackeroo, between 1929 and 1931, when he wrote the three 'obsessive novels', *The Immigrants, Finding Heaven* and *The Sullen Moon*, that have since disappeared; he wrote these at the farm dining-room table, much to the amazement of those around him. Cambridge too offered escape – as it did for Forster, another homosexual writer oppressed by convention. But in White's case liberation came from travels in France and Germany, not Italy and Greece. The sexual duality and ambivalence that pervades White's life and art even affects the way he recalls his Cambridge Modern Language studies in masculine French and feminine German. A more obvious duality is that felt between European culture and Australian nature as embodied in bush and desert. Eventually, after spending most of the thirty-six years of his life outside Australia, he returned in 1948 to satisfy a 'terrible nostalgia' and to escape becoming 'that most sterile of beings, a London intellectual' ('The Prodigal Son', p. 156); but not before immersing himself for many years in London artistic and theatrical circles. Through a close friendship with the painter Roy de Maistre he learnt to look for the core of reality beneath the surface – a clue to all his writing. And he spent practically all his time in the company of actors and haunting theatres. Before his return to Australia in 1948, when he had to adapt himself 'to what seemed a foreign country and a foreign language',[1] he had published two novels, *Happy Valley* (1939) and *The Living and the Dead* (1941); he completed a third, *The Aunt's Story* (1948), on his journey home.

Happy Valley and *The Living and the Dead*, the first set in rural Australia and the second in a London reminiscent of T. S. Eliot's 'unreal city', both express the author's painful struggle to discover meaning in an apparently meaningless universe. In *Happy Valley*, which was praised by Edwin Muir in England and was awarded a gold medal in Australia but which the author has deliberately allowed to go out of print, there is some confusion of purpose. The metaphysical theme and the sociological theme are logically incompatible. The first asserts that suffering is a universal and necessary precondition for spiritual progress, an idea embodied in the epigraph from Gandhi, 'the purer the suffering, the greater the progress'; the second suggests that suffering arises from local conditions and can either be remedied or escaped. Like many works of the 1930s, Thornton Wilder's *Our Town* (1938) for instance, the novel builds up a powerful composite image of the dreams and frustrations of small-town rural life.

This is a very literary first novel, which contains a soliloquy reminiscent of Molly Bloom, a Joycean sensitive schoolboy, and a very Lawrentian scene involving the death of a snake. In the climax, children play a crucial role, suggesting potentialities for harmony, as they often do in White's novels – a conception very different from that represented by the devouring faces of the baby-boom children in the late play *Signal Driver,* first staged in 1982. In *Happy Valley,* the unhappy schoolboy Rodney finds joy and harmony in the half-caste Margaret's company; and Margaret leaves her drunken, lecherous father and nagging mother to live with her uncle and aunt. As the hero, Dr Halliday, and his family drive away from the ironically named Happy Valley for the last time, the son Rodney sees Margaret and her uncle and aunt as a harmonious,

17

stoical group: 'Sometimes you thought that the Quongs were exotic, foreign to Happy Valley, but not as they stood outside the store, this first and last evidence of life' (*HV*, p. 326). Less convincing and more assertive is the hero's vision of the 'mystery of unity', after leaving his sleeping mistress (*HV*, p. 166). Here, and in the final paragraphs of the novel, the larger metaphysical theme appears contrived because insufficiently grounded in the given world of the fiction, a fault that sometimes recurs in later novels. But certainly *Happy Valley* is a striking study of small-town life, the stifled passions of its inhabitants and their desires for a wider life. They are caught up in its monotonous daily rhythms as are the suburban characters in White's fine expressionistic play, *The Season at Sarsaparilla* (1962).

White continues to grapple with the problem of suffering in his second novel, *The Living and the Dead* (1941). But he now extends this theme through the processes of doubling, multiplication and fragmentation. Instead of having a single figure in search of truth, he has a brother and a sister, Elyot and Eden Standish. Each is involved with contrasted potential partners and all the characters may be seen as fragments of a whole person. At the beginning and near the end, Elyot reflects: 'Alone, he was yet not alone, uniting as he did the themes of so many other lives' (*LD*, pp. 18, 357). This theme of psychic fragmentation and empathic unity has a strong personal basis: in an interview printed in *Southerly*, White remarked 'all my characters are fragments of my own somewhat fragmented character'[2] and in his autobiography he said of his cousin Marianne Wynne and the servants Lizzie, Matt and Flo, 'each is a fragment of my own character' (*FG*, p. 32). The theme of fragmentation is developed further in *The Aunt's Story*, in the dream fugues in the 'Jardin Exotique' (a garden which is a fictional analogue of Dufy's painting *Le Jardin d'hiver*), and in the heroine's confrontation with the composite figure of Holstius at the end of that novel. But she is an active quester, while Elyot Standish is more static – a Prufrock figure – whose reaction to the faces in the street is that 'the whole business was either a mystery, or else meaningless, and of the two, meaninglessness is the more difficult to take' (*LD*, p. 9). Yet he certainly longs for a purpose and vitality that would redeem his death-in-life existence in London, as do many of the others characters, including his sister and her working-class lover Joe, both of whom seek meaning in life through active participation in the Spanish civil war.

In the early short story 'The Twitching Colonel' and in the first two novels, private epiphanies play a crucial role. However, White is not always successful in investing the apparently trivial with transcendental significance. In *Happy Valley* a lustre bowl is required to serve too many symbolic purposes, while in *The Living and the Dead* Elyot's boyhood experience with the mandalic 'red and periwinkle stone' is never fully realized, so that the recurrence of the image in the climax fails to serve the intended purpose of marking a moment of wordless illumination for brother and sister as they part at the railway station. Already in these early works, White frequently plays on the idea that the highest form of communication is silence:

> so it boiled down to this, the folded hands, the ultimate simplicity of a room. I got to go, said Joe. I got to catch my train. . . . After groping behind the dry symbols of words, you experienced a sudden revelation in a shabby, insignificant room. (*LD*, p. 308)

Such wordless revelations as this between the hero and the handsome Joe, to whom he is physically attracted, become more and more common in White's fiction as he frees himself from the constraints of social realism. He first achieves this freedom – perhaps influenced by Alain-Fournier whose fantasy *Le Grand Meaulnes* he greatly admired – in *The Aunt's Story*, White's briefest and most perfectly composed novel.

The Aunt's Story is difficult but infinitely rewarding. Most of the difficulties disappear, however, once the reader recognizes its relationship to the novels of James Joyce and Virginia Woolf. The characteristics that it shares with this type of fiction

19

are the use of interior monologue, the extreme fluidity of movement from the inner thoughts of one character to another, the resolution of strict clock-time into the subtler mysteries of psychological time, the quest for psychic harmony through the creative exercise of memory, and the creation of significant patterns of meaning through the cumulative repetition of remembered images. A striking example of a time shift and exploration of consciousness through a remembered image occurs in the second part of the novel 'Jardin Exotique' when the deranged heroine, Theodora Goodman, relives the experience of a Greek earthquake. But the shift is not back into her own past but, through a process of imaginative empathy, into the past of another character, the young Greek girl Katina. The sequence begins with Katina's words 'There was an earthquake, do you remember?' (*AS*, p. 142) and ends with the same words a few pages later (p. 144). What occurs between is largely Theodora's imaginative experience of the moment of death as she identifies herself with Katina and becomes her protector. The reader is well prepared for Theodora's ability to identify with Katina and, indeed, with all the other eccentric characters by the epigraph to Part 2, 'Henceforward we walk split into myriad fragments', and also by the words that immediately precede the earthquake, 'And Theodora had become a mirror, held to the child's experience' (*AS*, p. 148). This idea of finding the self through gazing into mirrors or living through others recurs constantly in White's fiction.

The structural and narrative strategies are also linked to another mode, that of allegory. First, the novel develops its deeper meanings by systematic references to stories and myths outside itself: Theodora's spiritual odyssey is frequently linked with Homer's *Odyssey*. Second, the novel is allegoric in that it includes such typical elements as the quest, a series of symbolic encounters, dreams and visions. Third, throughout the work, the self of the heroine divides and fragments, so that the encounters with other people are to be interpreted, in part, as encounters with different facets of the self. But because this is a novel, the events and characters do not inhabit a complete fantasy world. Sokolnikov, who is actually based on 'a crazy White Russian' White had known, is a realistic character, a former Russian major posing as a general, as well as being a distorted image of Theodora's dead father. All the characters in this middle section of the novel have a dual dimension. They exist as independent characters and as allegoric representations of Theodora's quest for reality in a real world made up of illusion.

The one character who is wholly allegoric is Holstius. He is Theodora's composite image of all those characters who have seemed to represent wholeness and totality: her kind but ineffective father, the Syrian trader with whom she once 'walked outside a distinct world', the Man who was Given his Dinner, and the Greek musician Moraïtis. In the deserted house into which she has retreated but made her own in America, she conjures up the figure of Holstius, a name chosen both because the author had known a Holstius and because of its association in German with 'wood', and hence a bedrock reality.

> Her breath beat. The walls were bending outward under the pressure of the hateful fire. Then, when the table screamed under her nails, he said quietly, 'Ah, Theodora, you are torn in two.'
>
> 'What is it,' she asked in agony, 'you expect me to do or say?'
>
> 'I expect you to accept the two irreconcilable halves. Come,' he said, holding out his hand with the unperturbed veins. (AS, p. 277)

Holstius symbolizes the possibility of reconciling duality and achieving unity. This is White's master theme. All the novels present us with two worlds, material and spiritual; they present us with two scales of value; and the characters inhabit two planes of existence. His is pre-eminently a dualistic universe. Yet his main aim is to assert the unity of all things, and the possibility that his chosen elect may enjoy visions of such unity.[3]

21

Three critical questions need to be posed at this juncture. Is the basis of White's vision essentially pyschological or is it religious (a question posed by both Manfred Mackenzie and Patricia Morley and answered in rather different ways)?[4] Does White possess the artistry to make his visionary moments seem authentic, not only for his chosen elect but for the reasonably sympathetic reader? Does White give sufficient fictional authenticity to his lost or damned characters, those who are too materialistic, selfish and obtuse to see visions of unity and thus be saved, such as Theodora's hard, possessive mother and the worldly Una Russell in *The Aunt's Story*, the devilish pair Mrs Flack and Mrs Jolley in *Riders in the Chariot*, and the bookish, self-centred Waldo in *The Solid Mandala*? Like E. M. Forster, Patrick White is a secular salvationist, dividing his characters into the saved and the damned, but it is not always easy to know what it is that saves and what damns. This is not to suggest that White's judgement is personal and arbitrary or that he is the God of his own fictional universe (although in some sense every good novelist is). But it is to suggest that he had to work harder than novelists who accept existing systems. He admits that 'it is very difficult to try to convey a religious faith through symbols and situations which can be accepted today.'[5] Like Blake, he tends to turn established values upside down. Just as Blake's Heaven and Hell are a reversal of the Christian hierarchy, so White's saints are the world's outcasts and his sinners are those who triumph by worldly standards. Redemption or salvation, the novels seem to say, are open only to the insane, the lonely artist or social outcast. In some sense, White's vision is the final perversion of the Romantic dream, his great predecessors being Blake and Baudelaire.

Each of the three parts of *The Aunt's Story* has an epigraph. These define the leading themes and prepare the reader for what follows. The first, which comes from Olive Schreiner, expresses 'the narrowness of the limits within which a human soul may speak and be understood by its nearest of mental kin'. In the early pages we observe the distance that separates the deeply alienated Theodora from her family, both in middle age and when she was a girl. After the description of her mother's death and funeral there is a characteristic flashback into childhood. As a child, Theodora's closest companion is her father. He introduces her to the idea that there is another Meroë than the Australian house they live in, 'a dead place, in the black country of Ethiopia' (AS, p. 23). He thus feeds the young girl's imagination so that 'the legendary landscape became a fact' and he provides the inspiration for her later spiritual odyssey. With the mother, who exerts her powerful and devious influence over the whole family, there is little communication. Mrs Goodman treats the awkward, 'yellow' Theodora contemptuously and bestows all her love on the pretty, 'pink' Fanny. In order to understand why Theodora retreats into what appears semi-madness, it is useful to recall R. D. Laing's studies of family case histories, which suggest that what is labelled madness is often the only escape that a child has from psychotic parents or a psychologically constrictive environment.

In this beautifully modulated, lyric novel White uses certain images to differentiate the two sisters, associating Theodora with rose-light and the Blake-like spiritual insight into the worm within the bud, and Fanny with the superficial beauty of the rose, pretty colours and pink flesh. Recurrent imagery also serves to mark the crucial epiphanies in Theodora's experience. The most obvious example is the triple repetition of the hawk, first associated with Theodora's relationship with her father and then with her two potential suitors: Frank Parrott, who subsequently marries pretty Fanny; and the elderly, well-upholstered Huntly Clarkson. First she sees 'a little hawk, with a reddish-golden eye, that looked at her as he stood on the sheep's carcass'. Then she recalls her father's remark that 'death lasts for a long time', and identifies with the 'red eye' that 'spoke of worlds that were brief and fierce' (AS, p. 33). Her eye and the hawk's eye become one. She perceives the elemental contraries, without attempting to enter into judgment. Her vision brings the duality of nature into unity. The hawk image next returns when she pleads with the coarse, worldly Frank

Parrott not to shoot a little hawk because she remembers the earlier experience. Frank ignores her, shoots and misses. 'Now she took her gun. She took aim, and it was like aiming at her own red eye' (p. 71). Here Theodora murders a part of her own self. Afterwards, 'She felt exhausted, but there was no longer any pain. She was as negative as air' (p. 71). The third hawk incident, which takes place at a fair ground with Huntly Clarkson, is a conscious parody of the others. Theodora's action in shooting at a china duck, a further act of self-murder, is wholly appropriate to the moral and physical atmosphere of her elderly suitor's tasteless, over-furnished world. Theodora is only at home spiritually in a bare world; hence the affinity she feels with the Greek cellist, Moraïtis, who explains ' "Greece, you see, is a bare country. It is all bones." "Like Meroë," said Theodora' (p. 108). Although the reader may not always know how much weight to place on particular images, the pattern of recurrent imagery serves to contrast characters, develop themes, mark out stages in Theodora's spiritual odyssey and explore the nature of reality.

The epigraph to the second part of the novel comes from Henry Miller. 'Henceforward we walk split into myriad fragments . . . and all things melt into music and sorrow; we walk against a united world, asserting our dividedness. All things, as we walk, splitting with us into a myriad iridescent fragments. The great fragmentation of maturity' (p. 133). The novel's action now passes from Australia to a small hotel on the Mediterranean and we enter on the second stage in Theodora's geographic and spiritual odyssey. Whereas in the first part, 'Meroë', the contrast was between the worlds of innocence and experience, now the contrast is between Hell and experience. The Hotel du Midi becomes a condensed image of Europe between the wars, a waste land of emotional sterility and frustration. Critics have not stressed sufficiently the close relationship between the fragmentation of Theodora's inner world and the break-up of European society, the result of left-wing revolutions and right-wing totalitarian rule. When one of the visitors reports the news that 'The Führer is annexing somewhere else, and half America has turned to dust', and asks Theodora whether she will go or stay, she replies: 'Then you do sometimes relate the personal to the universal' (p. 232). The political context locates the heroine's otherwise homeless quest in a known historical world; her personal odyssey takes place against a background of social chaos and disintegration. Those she meets at the hotel are not only refugees from reality, absurd cherishers of mad dreams and illusions, but a cross-section of Europe's uprooted sufferers. In this baleful atmosphere her quest turns into an anti-quest, as Manfred Mackenzie has observed: 'she has to grope for a mock Grail, the nautilus, which disintegrates in the same way as "the gothic shell of Europe" will eventually disintegrate'. As a quester, she only has the choice between illusions of reality and the reality of illusions, and the nautilus is either or both.[6] Important as the historical and social dimensions of the 'Jardin Exotique' section are, it is vital to recognize how closely this part re-enacts the latent emotional content of the heroine's earlier years.

Because she is no longer constrained by conventional bonds, Theodora is free to liberate herself through her imaginative identification with the dreams, illusions and frustrated passions of the hotel residents. Katina is an image of her innocent self on the brink of experience, Sokolnikov of her father, Mrs Rapallo of her mother, and the destructive relations of Wetherby and Lieselotte are a more extreme repetition of her own earlier tortuous emotions. The struggle for the nautilus shell, the visit to the ruined tower, whose smell of nettles is associated with Theodora's first sight of guilty adult passions in childhood (cf. AS, pp. 238, 36), and the fire that destroys the hotel: all have potent symbolic resonance, though it would be foolish to assign a precise meaning to each. However, it is obviously significant that Theodora and Katina escape from the fire, that Katina walks out of the burning building 'with her hands outstretched, protecting herself with her hands, not so much from substance, as some other fire' (p. 250), and equally significant that they discover 'the lost reality of childhood' before Theodora sets out on the third stage of her odyssey.

The third section, 'Holstius', has the shortest epigraph. Again it comes from Olive Schreiner: 'When your life is most real, to me you are mad'. Theodora now moves to America. The vast expanses of corn through which the train moves suggest the simplicity and immensity of the spiritual world she has entered. The rustic simplicity she encounters when she abruptly leaves the train is in striking contrast to the empty luxury she has left behind in the Jardin Exotique. She has not only stripped herself of inessentials, but has come closer to humility, anonymity and purity of being. To some extent, the American country boy Zac now takes over the role of innocent initiator and guide formerly played by Katina. Once Theodora has learnt the wisdom of acceptance from the symbolic Holstius, she is restored to a state of being in which she is at one with the chair she sits on.

The quiet sense of final peace is movingly expressed in the closing pages. But the circumstantial details relating to the arrival of the doctor and Theodora's removal to an asylum draw excessive attention to the paradox stated in the epigraph 'When your life is most real, to me you are mad.' The ending is paradoxically too definite and too inconclusive: too definite in that the sanity/insanity paradox is so prosaically wound up in the plot; and too inconclusive in that the working out of the major theme seems to require that Theodora's new wholeness of vision should be more closely related with the scene of her childhood in Australia. The reader feels the need for some geographic return to Australia (real or imaginary) or alternatively some final fusion of the worlds of innocence and experience. But the total rejection of society that White's ending implies is completely in line with his later celebration of the sanity of his misunderstood solitaries and the insanity of the world – a celebration that reaches its logical conclusion in the play *Netherwood* (1983), where he dramatizes the conflicting values in a grand shoot-out between the representatives of a 'mad' society and the 'sane' patients in a private mental home.

The early works discussed in this chapter illustrate the fictional matrix from which all White's works spring. Its constituents are a belief in visionary experience and the redemptive power of love, the almost compulsive return to childhood experiences for illuminations and epiphanies, the creative exercise of memory, fragmentation as a necessary prelude to psychic harmony, ironic reversal of orthodox ideas of success and failure, sanity and madness; and, underlying all these, the lonely quest for truth, the core of being, which is hidden beneath the surface. In spite of the strong personal elements in this fictional matrix, the novels cannot be called autobiographical. The process by which White fragments his personality to live through the most unlikely characters makes it difficult, even in *The Aunt's Story*, for the reader to enjoy any easy identification with a privileged central figure. Such identification is quite impossible in the later novel, *The Solid Mandala* (1966), where he lives with equal imaginative intensity through the strongly contrasted twin brothers. The author's self is reflected and refracted in each novel as a whole, not in a single figure.

2

MIDDLE NOVELS: AUSTRALIAN EPICS

Patrick White's return to Australia in 1948 marks the main turning-point in his life and art. He describes ironically how at Castle Hill, a small-holding about 20 miles outside Sydney where he bred goats and dogs for several years, he fell on his back in the mud and knew that God had struck – just as He strikes so many of White's fictional elect, including Stan Parker, the hero of his next novel. The return also led to a changed conception of writing. 'Writing which had meant the practice of an art by a polished mind in civilized surroundings, became a struggle to create completely fresh forms out of rocks and sticks of words.' The result was the two Australian epics, *The Tree of Man* (1955) and *Voss* (1957). His motives in coming back to Australia were complicated, but included a 'longing to return to the scenes of childhood . . . the purest well from which the creative artist draws', 'a nostalgia for desert landscape', a desire to escape the fate of becoming a London intellectual, and the promised 'stimulus of time remembered'. These motives throw light on what he subsequently wrote, so too does his immediate reaction to 'the Great Australian Emptiness', in which, he suggests:

> mind is the least of possessions, in which the rich man is the important man, in which the schoolmaster and journalist rule what intellectual roost there is . . . and the march of material ugliness does not raise a quiver from the average nerves.

It was, indeed, the 'exaltation of the average' that made White 'panic most' but which also led him to conceive another novel, *The Tree of Man*, one of the main purposes of which would be to 'discover the extraordinary behind the ordinary, the mystery and poetry which alone could make bearable the lives of such people, and incidentally, my own life since my return'.[7]

In *The Tree of Man* – which started under the title 'A Life Sentence on Earth' – White took over and adapted the family saga of pioneering days which had been popularized by Brian Penton in *The Land Takers* (1934) and Katherine Susannah Prichard in her goldfields trilogy, and which is still immensely popular today, especially on television. But where such sagas focus on romatic love and melodramatic action, White's pastoral epic combines a simple, Genesis-style creation myth with a sensitive exploration of man's spiritual struggle. In *The Rainbow* (1915), D. H. Lawrence had already shown how the familiar family chronicle could be adapted to dramatize spiritual and erotic conflicts; he had shown how the family saga could be internalized so that the stress fell on states of feeling, not external events. But White's choice of inarticulate main characters offers an additional challenge that is not always met; nevertheless, this choice is completely in line with his frequent affirmation that words come between man and reality, that silence is a necessary precondition for vision and wisdom.

Stan Parker, the inarticulate hero, appears on the opening page as the anonymous archetypal pioneer. Accompanied by his red dog, he clears the bush with vigorous strokes and eats his tucker by the camp-fire; then the eyes of man and dog and horse make up 'a unity of eyes and firelight' (*TM*, p. 10). In these early pages the imagery and simple, biblical rhythms reinforce the sense of an antipodean creation myth. 'The Man struck at the tree, and struck, till several white chips had fallen. He looked at the scar in the side of the tree. The silence was immense. It was the first time anything like this happened in that part of the bush' (p. 9). Although Stan's mother wanted him to be a teacher or a preacher, he emerges as the type of man

29

who finds meaning through physical action and silent communion with nature. The novel traces his battles with fire, flood and drought; the stages of his marriage to Amy; the fates of his children and grandchildren; the gradual incursion of suburban ugliness and mediocrity into his pastoral Eden (a fictional analogue to White's experience at Castle Hill); and his final moment of illumination when, just before his death, he is granted a vision of the unity of all things with himself at the centre.

At first, Amy's subordination to Stan seems appropriate to the Old Testament ethos created in the opening pages – he becomes 'her only God', and the man 'consumed the woman'; but subsequently she suffers a gratuitous moral decline with her unexpected and improbable adultery with Leo, the commercial traveller. It is as if the elevation of the male requires a corresponding degradation of the female. This pattern, which recurs in later novels, also affects the minor characters, such as the daughter Thelma and the beautiful, romantic Madeleine, who is transformed into the social mediocrity, Mrs Fisher.

More satisfactory in the structure of the novel is the contrast that is consistently developed between Stan's and Amy's responses to experience. Broadly speaking, Stan is responsive to the indefinable mystery of life, while Amy looks for some tangible evidence of such 'otherness'. Stan is capable of reconciling the quest for permanence with the necessity for change, while Amy longs only for permanence. Until Amy's adultery with Leo, the radically opposed responses to experience appear equally valid; thereafter Amy's are consistently downgraded and she is condemned as unworthy of Stan:

> as she watched this erect and honourable man she realized with blinding clarity that she had never been worthy of him. . . . In time the knowledge that some mystery was withheld from her ceased to make her angry, or miserable for her own void. (pp. 317–18)

Storms, floods, fires and droughts, which are the distinctive elements in tales of the Australian bush, serve to signal import-

30

ant stages in the relationship of husband and wife and in their contrasted responses to the 'otherness' of nature. For example, the storm in Chapter 5 brings Stan and Amy together in a new unity, after the arrival of other people in the district has threatened their relationship. Stan craves solitude and Amy, society. In the storm they regain a naked innocence and a new understanding of their dependence on each other. But as yet Stan cannot penetrate 'the mystery of the natural world'; and White adds the proleptic sentence: 'Only sometimes the touch of hands, the lifting of a silence, the sudden shape of a tree or presence of a first star, hinted at eventual release' (*TM*, p. 49).

The description of the Wullunya flood and the fire that destroys the retired pork butcher's house, Glastonbury, are both elaborate set-pieces and integral parts of the thematic design. In each, White combines graphic details with fairy-tale motifs and symbolism. The incident of the boy whom the Parkers rescue from the flood and temporarily adopt but who mysteriously disappears, belongs to fairy-tale, as does the romantic horsewoman, Madeleine, whom Amy sends her husband to rescue from the burning Glastonbury House. For Amy, the fire is a practical threat to life; for Stan it is much more. His encounter with the red-haired Madeleine in the burning house is his first experience of the flames of a potentially ennobling but devouring passion. The two 'burnt ones' can never be the same again. 'It was not their flesh that touched but their final bones. Then they were writhing through the fire. . . . When her teeth fastened in his cheek it expressed their same agony' (*TM*, p. 180). For years Stan retains the memory of this intense, devouring passion – the kind that consumed Wetherby and Lieselotte in the Hotel du Midi fire in *The Aunt's Story*. But Amy dismisses the image of Madeleine as a figure from a novelette. The Madeleine episode reveals Stan's incapacity to respond fully to an elemental passion that is both destructive and potentially purifying; it also reveals Amy's limited imagination: '"She was frightened, poor thing," she said looking at him through the darkness. "Such an experience"' (*TM*, p. 182). The staging of the whole episode is ambiguous. The reader is likely to share Amy's view that the image of Madeleine is novelettish, yet she was based on one of the author's cousins, 'who crossed the mountain' to register her protest at White's manner of writing and to ask a former servant of the White family 'Does he think he's pulling our legs?' (*FG*, p. 31).

It is not only through Stan and Amy that White explores contrasted approaches to truth. The lives of their neighbours provide variations and alternatives. The slatternly Irish woman Mrs O'Dowd, married to a hopeless drunk, has a generous warmth and easy tolerance that Amy lacks, and Amy's confession that she had 'no understanding' of her friend Mrs O'Dowd's death defines the limitations of her sympathy and human understanding. Doll Quigley and her simpleton brother Bub personify two other basic responses to life. Bub, one of White's many divine fools, sees into the heart of things, much to the embarrassment of others; he recognizes instinctively the goodness of the dead man suspended upside down in a tree in the Wullunya flood and wishes to touch him (White recently said he would like to have been that suspended man). Doll is the embodiment of natural goodness and intuitive wisdom, like Mrs Godbold in *Riders in the Chariot* and White's childhood servants who, he felt, were his real parents and true source of love and affection (*FG*, pp. 14, 30). Doll's actions obey natural instincts, not social conventions. When she explains what has happened to her brother Bub, she says: 'I put him away. I will not say kill. Because I loved Bub' (*TM*, p. 464). Such directness clearly shows up Amy, 'the confused woman of ant-proportions, even smelling of ants' (p. 464); yet Stan includes the ants in his final vision when 'he was illuminated', and even Amy is granted a degree of self-knowledge and becoming humility. After thinking conventionally that Doll 'was in hell', she says: 'We suffer for some purpose . . . but I am one of the stupid ones. I could not answer Mrs O'Dowd either, when the time came' (p. 465).

Since this is a family saga the reader is concerned with the lives of the Parkers' children and grandchildren as well as with Stan and Amy. The continuation of the narrative into the two younger generations enables White to present aspects of Australian suburban life that he found distasteful on his return from England. But this produces a disturbing change in tone and intention in the last third of the novel. The son Ray becomes a petty criminal and dies in a sordid shoot-out, the daughter Thelma makes a respectable marriage and comes to epitomize the superficiality and gentility that White increasingly satirizes in his later novels, plays and short stories. If the lives of Stan and Amy's children are a failure, the grandson Ray appears – however improbably – as the potential poet who will 'write a poem of life, of all life, of what he did not know, but knew' (*TM*, p. 480). In other words, he will write a work like *The Tree of Man*. In contrast to the free creative flow of the first two-thirds, much of the writing in the last third is too consciously willed. The satirical passages are heavy-handed and Stan's final vision of God in a gob of spittle is too artfully juxtaposed with the confident vacuities of the young evangelist who promises Stan the 'glories of salvation' if he will repent his sins.

In *The Tree of Man*, as in most of White's fiction, all the characters are fragments and variations of the author's self: 'All the characters in my books are myself, but they are a kind of disguise.' The novel celebrates two antithetical responses to life: on the one hand, the virtues of apartness and mystic intuition; and on the other, the virtues of loving-kindness and community. For much of the time there is a dynamic tension between the two; but eventually the chronicle affirms the superiority of the former, the way of the elect. Yet there is a radical difference between the endings of *The Aunt's Story* and *The Tree of Man*. Where Theodora Goodman comes to enjoy an other-worldly transcendence, Stan Parker discovers the divine in nature and in common objects. White's own joy in the 'refreshed landscape' on his return to Australia irradiates his description of the natural world. With Stan Parker he begins to know 'every corner of darkness, as if it were daylight, and he were in love with the heaving world, down to the last blade of wet grass' (*TM*, p. 151). From now on White paints the natural

33

and man-made world of Australia with the soul of a poet and the brush of a great romantic expressionist artist; Nolan's cover designs have helped to mediate this vision to readers.

The other dynamic tension, between the masculine and the feminine elements in the author's psyche, is not so well sustained. It is only in the late novel, *The Twyborn Affair* (1979) that White can fully dramatize the importance of recognizing 'the woman in man and the man in woman'. In the relatively early novel, *The Tree of Man*, he splits the feminine into two, undervaluing the social woman and sentimentalizing the natural, instinctive woman embodied in Mrs O'Dowd, Mrs Quigley and Lolo – Ray Parker's *de facto* wife. Lolo, whose creation probably owes something to Puccini and to the colourful Lola Montez, is the only woman Stan learns from. When he visits her briefly after the death of his son, he observes her acceptance of the 'necessary slavery' of motherhood. On his return home, he sees his aged wife Amy in a new light: he sees the 'thin girl encased in this comfortable old woman' and he is 'cut open by the poignance of it' (*TM*, p. 442). Clearly, White means us to see that both Stan and Lolo are 'burnt ones' and that their mutual illumination is the product of intense suffering; but the crucial scene carries less than full conviction, because Lolo is a sentimental stereotype and the dialogue is stilted and assertive. Why, the reader asks, does Stan require a Lolo to open his eyes when he has spent a lifetime of joys and sorrows with Amy? After the vast splendours of the earlier epic narrative it is unfortunate that the narrator's manipulative hand should be so evident towards the end.

*

The Tree of Man and *Voss* (1957) are both based on the metaphor of life as a journey, a favourite metaphor in much Australian writing for obvious historical and geographical reasons. In *The Tree of Man* Stan Parker's journey is through time; in *Voss* the hero's journey is through space. In both novels, the temporal and spatial voyages are in essence spiritual ones, although the actual details of Stan's pioneering life and

34

Voss's blundering but heroic exploration are rendered with absolute fidelity to physical fact and sensuous experience. In both novels White's desire to break away from the kind of fiction that is 'the dreary dun-coloured offspring of journalistic realism' and give his prose 'the textures of music, the sensuousness of paint' is triumphantly realized.[8] Critics who have praised White for endowing the landscape with visionary horror in the later stages of Voss's journey into the Dead Heart have not sufficiently recognized the simple authenticity of the earlier descriptions. Nor have they always noticed the acute distinction between the attitudes towards the land exhibited by Mr Bonner, Mr Sanderson and Mr Boyle. Each attitude is different and each typifies a social class in early colonial society. Mr Bonner typifies the materialistic attitude of the successful merchant, Mr Sanderson the pastoral idealism of the educated settler who sought a new Arcady in Australia, and Mr Boyle the careless indifference of the Irish ne'er-do-well.

Voss is a novel rich in mythic and symbolic meanings, but how well these are articulated and controlled is still as much a matter of debate as when James McAuley and G. A. Wilkes assessed the novel soon after its first publication.[9] White had read the Australian explorer Edward John Eyre's *Journal* during the bombing in London and, on his return to Australia, he read the story of Leichhardt's disastrous last expedition in A. H. Chisholm's *Strange New World*: both contributed much to the novel. Three seminal suggestions came from his wartime experiences: the first from his feelings about 'that archmegalomaniac' Hitler, who typified for him, as Voss does at another level, the tragic consequences of the insane assertion of the human will; the second from his own desert wanderings as an Intelligence Officer in the RAF; and the third from his experience of censoring airmen's mail. The outpourings of servicemen separated by thousands of miles from their loved ones provided the initial inspiration for the Voss/Laura relationship. Here was simple proof that love could vanquish separation, that a natural affinity of minds could conquer distance. The theme of Voss is the testing of the self-sufficient will through confrontation with the Australian outback and the discovery of the need for love.

The natural affinity between Laura and Voss is firmly established at the outset. For the success of the novel, it is important that the reader should recognize the two levels of Laura's response to the ill-dressed, arrogant German explorer, Voss, whose arrival is announced on the first page by the maid: '"There is a man here, miss, asking for your uncle," said Rose Portion. And stood breathing.' At the social level, Laura acts like a well-brought-up nineteenth-century lady, dispensing conversation and the second-best port. At a deeper level, she feels a strong affinity with Voss. The fact that in this first meeting she 'could hear her own voice' in Voss's establishes this affinity. The social self, however, reasserts itself as Laura becomes tired of 'this enclosed man' and imagines the words she would use to meet a proposal from Voss, as she had prepared answers for two previous proposals that had never quite eventuated. Yet in spite of this reassertion of the social self, the sense of a secret affinity, a shared subterranean life, has been firmly established. This sense of a silent spiritual communion re-emerges at the picnic party described in the third chapter: 'both man and woman were lulled into living inwardly, without shame or need of protection' (p. 69). But the experience does not blind Laura to Voss's faults and she rebukes him by saying that 'this expedition of yours is pure will'. In reply Voss makes a remark that foreshadows the whole pattern of their relationship, based as it will be on absence, and on a kind of mental telepathy or shared spiritual hallucination. '"Your interest is touching, Miss Trevelyan," he laughed, "I shall appreciate it in many desert places"' (p. 69).

The opening scenes establish this secret understanding between Voss and Laura; they also build up a strong contrast between the complacent worldliness of the early colonial settlers and the other-worldly idealism of Voss. The chief sponsor of the expedition, Mr Bonner, consistently uses metaphors of the counting house, while Voss enjoys mandalic visions, 'looking at each word as if it were a round pebble of mystical perfection' (p. 20). The mandala, which is one of White's most frequently recurring images and provides the title for one novel (*The Solid Mandala*), is a sacred or magical diagram. Composed of circles and squares, it represents wholeness or perfection and is used for purposes of meditation in various eastern religions.

Certainly Voss is the central mandalic figure in this poetic novel and his fateful expedition is the means of exploring the strengths and limitations of the Nietzschean 'Superman' whose task it is to fill the void that arises from the idea that 'God is dead'. But concentration on Voss is not at the expense of his companions in the quest, all of whom have a representative stature that is both historical and symbolic. Historically Leichhardt's expedition was made up of just such people: 'an ornithologist; a convict; a somewhat delicate youth of nineteen whom the leader met on board ship . . . a boy of fifteen who was also a shipboard acquaintance; another Englishman; a young squatter; and two aboriginals.'[10] In Leichhardt's party Gilbert, like Palfreyman in Voss's, was both ornithologist and artist. Indeed, the Australian explorers drew on two traditions. On the one hand, they drew on the European Enlightenment in their scientific devotion to collecting accurate information about the unknown flora and fauna, working under instructions first laid down by the Royal Society; on the other hand, they drew on the Romantic tradition in their search for the exotic, in their response to wild, uncharted beauty, and in their typically romantic wish to escape from society and dedicate themselves to some lonely, heroic quest.

The various characters in *Voss* suggest different approaches to the quest for truth. Voss represents the Nietzschean 'Superman', whose confidence in his own powers and willingness to sacrifice others borders on megalomania. Frank Le Mesurier is the doomed poet, created on the model of the French symbolist poet Rimbaud, a type that recurs later in a more developed form in Hurtle Duffield in *The Vivisector*. The latter novel actually uses a quotation from Rimbaud as an epigraph: 'He becomes beyond all others the great invalid, the great Criminal, the great Accursed One – and the Supreme Knower. For he reaches the Unknown.' Even though Frank Le Mesurier is only a small-scale model of the type, he certainly strives to reach the unknown and appears 'doomed' from the start. His words, when Voss invited him to join the expedition, foreshadow the exact nature of his suicide: 'No . . . I'm not sure I want to cut my throat just yet' (V, p. 34). Like Rimbaud, Le Mesurier expresses his visions in prose poems. These provide clues to his poetic quest. Voss reads one of them but dismisses it as self-indulgent romanticism, even though it is applicable to his own relationship with Laura: 'We do not meet but in distances, and dreams are the distance brought close' (V, p. 295). Voss also scorns Le Mesurier's humility because it denies the royal supremacy of the will. But it is Palfreyman, the artist on the expedition, who most fully personifies Christian humility. As the exact antithesis of Voss, he cultivates the virtues of charity, patience and humility. These are qualities that Voss dismisses as irrelevant but which he exploits when he virtually sends Palfreyman to his death. This death represents the victory of one man's proud, assertive will over another's Christian humility.

The spirit of joyful amity and expectation in which the expedition sets out from Rhine Towers, 'when the very stirrup-irons were singing of personal hopes' (p. 154), is in marked contrast to the bitter dissensions that break out. As the details of the exploration unfold it is clear that Voss's party must divide. On the one hand are the visionaries, such as Voss, Palfreyman, Le Mesurier, Harry and Jackie; on the other hand are the realists, such as the emancipist Judd, who becomes the leader of the breakaway party, the crude, bawdy materialist Turner, and his new friend, the young grazier Ralph Angus. What mainly precipitates the division into Voss's and Judd's parties is Judd's wish to celebrate Christmas. This Voss dismisses as a desecration of a holy shrine – the shrine made holy by himself. He protests angrily, 'Yet, to drag in the miserable fetish that this man has insisted on! Of Jesus Christ!' (p. 197). Voss considers himself superior to Christ who typifies a contemptible humility in his eyes. As he watches Judd in the centre of a worshipping circle he recalls that once he and Laura had made a circle of their own: 'As he saw it now, perfection is always circular, enclosed. So that Judd's circle was enviable' (p. 198). Enclosed within his own proud selfhood, Voss rejects social relations and all gestures signifying human brotherhood. 'Left alone, Voss groaned. He would not, could not learn, nor accept humility, even though this was amongst the conditions she had made in the letter that was now living in him' (p. 199).

What is unconvincing in the conception of Voss is the sudden leap from insane egoism to selfless love. The crucial scene occurs in section 13. After Frank has committed suicide, the proud explorer Voss and the faithful simpleton Harry Roberts are drawn together.

> As the two fell into sleep, or such a numb physical state as approximated to it, Voss believed that he loved this boy, and with him all men, even those he hated, which is the most difficult act of love to accomplish, because of one's own fault. (p. 382)

This is psychologically implausible since nothing prepares us for it. More convincing are the passages in which Voss feels the loving presence of Laura so vividly that it is obvious that 'she must be at his side and, in fact, he heard a second horse blowing out its nostrils' (p. 392). Under her influence Voss transforms the desert into an Edenic landscape and it is in this 'luminous state of consciousness' that he meets 'the supreme emergency with strength and resignation': the Aboriginal Jackie stabs him and cuts off his head. 'His dreams fled into the air, his blood ran out upon the dry earth, which drank it up immediately' (p. 394). Voss's death is here conceived partly in relation to Aboriginal myths about man's spirit returning to the earth.

The last part of the novel illustrates the various distortions that a death and a myth can breed. In a tightly packed narrative there is no sense of haste as the action moves easily between Sydney and the outback, and the present and the past. Two major episodes provide ironic perspectives on the hero. The first, Laura's interview with Colonel Hepden, who is as obstinate and self-willed as Voss but lacks the German's heroic vision, establishes firmly the duality of Voss in Laura's mind, that 'Voss could have been the Devil' (*V*, p. 414). The second, the scene at Belle Radclyffe's party, is a fine example of White's virtuosity in shifting the focus in the last phases of his fictions. Each of Belle's guests, figures from the past like herself, contributes something vital to the reassessment of the German explorer, especially those who come on from the unveiling ceremony. Much play is made of Voss's ironic transformation into a public hero and potent myth 'hung with garlands of rarest newspaper prose'. But the supreme irony is that the sole survivor of the expedition, Judd, confuses the circumstances of Voss's death with Palfreyman's. He comes closer to reality when he says, 'Voss? No. He was never God, though he liked to think that he was. Sometimes, when he forgot, he was a man' (p. 443). He promptly spoils all this with sentimental gush about the explorer's being a Christian, which appals Laura and also the reader, since the overlay of Christian symbolism in the epiphanies can only impress those insensitive to falsities of tone and texture. Laura's assertion that Voss 'did not die' needs to be seen in its ironic context as a rhetorical boast prompted by the disparaging remarks of a drunken English visitor: '"Voss did not die," replied Miss Trevelyan. "He is there still, it is said, in the country, and always will be. His legend will be written down, eventually, by those who have been troubled by it"' (p. 448). Her words are not the ringing affirmation they might be in a less ironic context. The last sentence of the novel preserves the ironic tone: 'By which time she had grown hoarse, and fell to wondering aloud whether she had brought her lozenges.' The voice of prophecy does not normally resort to throat lozenges.

Of course Voss's legend is written down; it is given a kind of immortality by being inscribed in the narrative text. It is the novelist who has been troubled by it and who explores, heroically and ironically, the fundamental ambiguity in Voss: was he god or devil? success or failure? Because the narrative is ironic and open-ended it is particularly important not to impose a facile Christian interpretation on his quest, not to interpret it as an exemplification of the simple idea that enters Laura's hallucinated mind about the three stages 'Of God into Man. Man. And Man returns to God' (*V*, p. 386), because the narrative will not sustain such a naïve interpretation.[11] In the novel as a whole Voss is revealed as the prisoner of his own selfhood who finds only partial release through his heroic encounter with the Australian landscape and through his reluctant and grudging initiation into the selfless world of love through Laura Trevelyan.

3

MIDDLE NOVELS:
ARTISTS AND VISIONARIES

White's next three novels, *Riders in the Chariot* (1961), *The Solid Mandala* (1966) and *The Vivisector* (1970), all focus on the transfiguring experiences of lonely visionaries and artists. In the two preceding novels, *The Tree of Man* and *Voss*, he had celebrated his rediscovery of the Australian landscape and explored the theme of the lonely, heroic quest through the very different lives of Stan Parker and Voss, both of whom search for ultimate meaning within the world and not beyond it. The novels of the next decade are primarily concerned with asserting the supremacy of feeling over intellect and with establishing the connection between suffering and spiritual insight, as this affects both artists and 'ordinary ones'. The artist figure gradually assumes a more important role. In *Riders in the Chariot*, Alf Dubbo's paintings mediate the meaning of Himmelfarb's mock crucifixion and death; in *The Solid Mandala*, Arthur Brown possesses the artist's seeing eye; and in *The Vivisector* Patrick White places the artist figure Hurtle Duffield in the centre of the fictional world and explores the implications of the idea of the artist as both creator and justified destroyer.

The epigraph to *Riders in the Chariot* is taken from Blake's poem, 'The Marriage of Heaven and Hell', and immediately suggests that this novel will celebrate the power of the spiritually elect to discover 'the infinite in everything' and hold out the promise of 'raising other men into a perception of the infinite'. Blake's words, 'the voice of honest indignation is the voice of God', foreshadow the sometimes uneasy blend of prophecy and savage satire that characterizes some parts of the novel. The actual title signifies that we are about to read a visionary novel that draws its central symbol from a passage in the Book of Ezekiel (1: 4–28) which Himmelfarb actually reads during a tea break in the Brighta Bicycle Lamp Factory (*RC*, p. 309).

Each of the four main characters comes to be seen as a Rider in the fiery Chariot of God: the lonely spinster Miss Hare, the German refugee intellectual Himmelfarb, the kindly, fecund Mrs Godbold and the doomed Aboriginal artist Alf Dubbo. Each enjoys a different vision of the Chariot. Because their lives form almost separate novels, it is necessary that they should be linked early on. In the first section of the novel, Miss Hare meets each of the Riders briefly. At this stage – and perhaps even to the end – it is not clear whether it is the potential for moments of illumination that links them or an awareness of their common humanity. In Miss Hare's meeting with Alf Dubbo it is clearly the first: 'Both the illuminates remained peacefully folded inside the envelopes of their flesh' (*RC*, p. 63). But in her first encounter with Himmelfarb the initial bond is their sense of a common humanity, although later in Himmelfarb's narrative she interjects: 'You know about the Chariot then' (p. 153). Flashes of illumination strengthen the bond. Yet it is Himmelfarb's physical presence and his tale of persecution and suffering that draw Miss Hare out of solitary, semi-mystical union with nature to embrace a larger world of suffering. In Ruth Godbold, other-worldly and human values are more specifically linked. White stresses the earthly basis of Ruth's apocalyptic vision, describing the wheels of her Chariot as 'solid gold, well-axled, as might have been expected' (p. 67). At this stage, it is worth raising the question whether White's attitude towards the capacity for vision and the capacity for love is muddled; also the question whether his prose is adequate to convey the mysterious sense of communion felt by the four Riders.

The meeting with Dubbo is particularly illuminating in this

respect. The first tentative movements of Miss Hare and Dubbo towards each other are conveyed through prose that is genuinely vital and explorative:

> So she would peer out at her dark man on these occasions when he walked through the lanes which ran past Xanadu. Once she had entered through his eyes, and at first glance recognized familiar furniture, and once again she had entered in, and their souls had stroked each other with reassuring feathers, but very briefly, for each had suddenly taken fright. (p. 62)

Here the active verbs, the bodily metaphors and subtle rhythms realize the experience fully. By contrast the passage that describes Miss Hare and Dubbo as 'illuminates' and 'apostles of truth' is over-assertive in language and tone. Indeed, the gap between authentically realized experience and apocalyptic experience is often very wide; the element of contrivance in the willed visionary encounters and climaxes shows through in the strained, over-affirmatory prose. There is also some discrepancy between the glad tidings announced by the grand, archetypal structures and the grim truths declared by the texture of the contorted, feverish prose.

In the stories of the four Riders, there is a very characteristic movement in the narrative from adult present to childhood past. The story of Miss Hare is that of a lonely, loveless childhood spent in the house called Xanadu where she was dominated by an eccentric, passionate father and a coldly conventional mother. The house – a false paradise – is her father's attempt to triumph over the 'grey dispiriting Australian landscape'. Three melodramatic encounters between father and daughter are formative for Mary. In the first, during an alcoholic bout, Norbert Hare suddenly cries out 'who are the riders in the Chariot, eh, Mary? Who is ever going to know?' (p. 23). In the second, when Norbert shoots at the chandeliers so loved by Mary, the father's attempts to destroy his daughter's innocence and engulf her in his own tragedy fail because she refuses to fall victim to his verbal menace, saying:

'But the truth is what I understand. Not in words. I have not the gift for words. But know' (p. 36). The third incident is the terrible confrontation before the father's histrionic suicide, which reveals the extent to which father and daughter have been locked in a life and death struggle. The macabre account of Norbert's reluctant suicide by drowning in the garden cistern has a grotesque, Dickensian power and ambiguity. Each has a dual vision of the other. To Mary, her drowning father is both an image of fearful awe and a comic, dog-like figure. To Norbert, Mary is both a potential saviour, 'Get some-thing, Mar-y!', and also a monstrous torturer and destroyer, when his own guilt and hatred make him see the pole that she proffers as an instrument of retribution, not deliverance, 'Mary! Don't. Have some pity!' (p. 57). The exploitation of dramatic perspective and the parallelism of Norbert's two cries throw into relief the duality of the father and daughter in each other's lives. Moreover, the interweaving of past and present makes Miss Hare's present state more intelligible. 'Her exorcising journey of rediscovery' reveals the continuity between the ugly, awkward little girl, alienated from people but loving animals, and the elderly spinster who wanders through the grounds of Xanadu dressed in earth-coloured stockings and great wicker sunflower hat and who enjoys a mystic sense of union with the divine in nature although appearing mad to the outside world. The narrative interweaving also heightens the contrast between the paradisal potentialities of Xanadu and the entry into that world of positive evil in the form of Mrs Flack and Mrs Jolley.

Of the four stories brought together in the novel, Himmelfarb's is the most humanly moving and artistically unified, except in the mock-crucifixion scene when Himmelfarb's Australian workmates string him up as a joke. Realism and archetypal symbolism fuse more naturally than in the stories of Ruth Godbold and Alf Dubbo. In the narrative of Himmelfarb's life all the separate elements cohere into a significant pattern of innocence, experience, suffering and redemption that seems to arise naturally from a densely created historical world. Within the German Jewish context, the idea of God's elect and of suffering persecution for truth's sake are not personal and idiosyncratic as they are with Miss Hare and Mrs Godbold; they are related to the world view of a large historical group. Specifically they are related to the idea of the Messiah, the *zaddik* (the thirty-six chosen holy men) and the biblical account of the persecution of the Jews in Egypt. The story of Himmelfarb's education in the Jewish faith, the early promise that he was destined to be the Messiah or one of the *zaddik*, when the Rabbi 'of almost womanly hands was searching his forehead for a sign', his bondage in Germany, his suffering and persecution as a Jew, his desire to atone for what he considered his desertion of his wife and people, his search for the Promised Land, his gradual rejection of the way of the intellect for redemption through suffering and love: all these major phases in the narrative are humanly credible and strongly charged with spiritual significance. The gap between signifier and signified, between the event and the high meaning attributed to it, is minimal. In the case of Ruth Godbold – a fat-rumped maternal figure who might have stepped out of a Stanley Spencer canvas – the gap between homely mother and modern saint is extreme and barely bridged.

Alf Dubbo's role in *Riders in the Chariot* is to serve as a seeing eye. He is the visionary artist who through suffering achieves the power to harmonize inner and outer worlds in paint. 'Neither the actor, nor the spectator, he was that most miserable of human beings, the artist' (*RC*, p. 407). It is the sexually exploited, diseased and dying Dubbo who realizes in paint the religious symbolism of Himmelfarb's death on the jacaranda tree and the associated iconography of the death-bed gathering in Mrs Godbold's shack, where Mrs Godbold becomes the first Mary, Miss Hare the 'Second Mary curled, like a ring-tail possum, in a dreamtime womb of transparent skin', Else the third Mary, and the children the watchers (*RC*, pp. 455–6). For Dubbo to fulfil his role, it is necessary for him to possess a knowledge of Christian iconography and an instinctive insight into the meaning of love and suffering. The unfolding of his past life, which includes a Christian education and social and sexual exploitation, shows how he acquired the appropriate experience. Even if there is some sense of cultural displacement as White adapts the European stereotype of the doomed Romantic artist to the largely uneducated Aboriginal, the frustrated pictorial artist in White finds triumphant expression in the painterly images that embody Dubbo's vision. His last painting serves the supremely important function of offering an image that reconciles the eternal conflict between permanence and motion, a central preoccupation in all White's fiction. 'From certain angles the canvas presented a reversal of the relationship between permanence and motion, as though the banks of a river were to begin to flow alongside its stationary waters' (*RC*, p. 458). The painting reconciles the conflict between body and spirit in its conception of the horses, both '*earthbound*' yet also touched with 'heavenly gold'. It offers condensed images of the four Riders in painterly form: Mrs Godbold as 'marble massive, white, inviolable'; Himmelfarb 'conceived in wire, with a star inside a cage, and a crown of barbed wire', Miss Hare with a 'harsh fox-coloured coat' and 'eye that reflected all that was ever likely to happen', and Dubbo constructed of 'Bleeding twigs and spattered leaves', but the head a 'whirling spectrum'. In its emphasis on the 'chariot-sociable', the picture also suggests a unity of humanity and other-worldliness. Dubbo's story ends with the appropriate irony that after his death, his expressive paintings are sold for next to nothing at auction and then disappear.

The pattern of each life is marked out by four stages: innocence, experience, suffering and redemption. The passage from innocence to experience varies considerably from one Rider to another, but in each case it is associated with some obscure sense of guilt and desertion and with a failure to integrate the conflicting masculine and feminine sides of the self, resulting in the 'death', real or symbolic, of the 'other', the buried self. Each of the Riders passes from the world of innocence to experience as a result of suffering, but again its actual origin is different in each case. The three characters who are subject to the greatest pressures retain their sanity; Mary Hare, the 'divine fool', does not; for her, the inner world alone is real, while for the others the outer world is both real and a cause of what they are. Each has personal knowledge of the Chariot, each can recognize the other as an 'apostle of truth', all sustain the paradox of strength in weakness and all are sacerdotal figures, engaged from time to time in performing simple rites. Ultimately all achieve the transition from mere existence to pure being. The unifying structure of *Riders in the Chariot* does not depend wholly on this common pattern of experience or on interwoven threads of the plot or on the sustained religious analogies. Without a related pattern of imagery, the sense of unity would be altogether weaker. Chain imagery differentiates communities of good from collusions of evil; the image of the circle constantly suggests the possibilities of perfection; and there is an obvious analogy between the destruction of the false paradise Xanadu which leads to youthful hope in later generations, and the annihilation of selfhood which must precede the transformations of the self. In an apocalyptic work, as we would expect, the elemental images of fire, air and water are supremely important. Most pervasive in developing White's vision of life is the parodic imagery that defines evil as a grotesque distortion of good. Thus Mrs Jolley's 'obscene', 'lethal' dance through the rooms and passages of Xanadu (*RC*, pp. 85–7) is at once a grotesque parody of the dances of Miss Hare's youth and of the elderly spinster's instinctive participation in the 'rite of the birds' (p. 38), where 'all throats were moving, wobbling, and hers most of all. In agreement.'

Yet in spite of the imaginative energy and resourcefulness expended in creating a sense of the unity of all things, there is a continuous conflict between the positive and negative sides of White's vision in *Riders in the Chariot*, between his compassionate sympathy with his elect and his distaste for humanity *en masse*. ('I wouldn't call myself a humanist. I am indifferent to people in general.'[12]) One might say that he was being true to the polarities of existence and that this imparts a dramatic

48

tension to his fiction. But, because the positive elements are so idiosyncratic and wilfully affirmed and the negative so emotionally overcharged, the polarities become those not of life but of the author's anguished psyche. The structure of the novel affirms salvation through the senses; the texture shudders and vibrates with physical loathing. What especially disturbs the balance and unity of the novel is the sense of moral outrage prompted by the outward manifestations of Australian suburbia, its drab uniformity, its plastic embellishments, its tasteless gentility, and the thoughtless cruelty that constantly threatens to erupt, as in the mock-crucifixion scene.

One effect of the displacement of so much imaginative energy into rendering the pink and plastic externals of Australian suburbia is to reduce its inhabitants to social automata. This makes it difficult for the reader to know how morally responsible such characters as Mrs Flack and Mrs Jolley and the Rosetrees are supposed to be. They and their world receive summary judgement from their omnipotent and outraged creator. And the redemption and salvation granted the elect is almost equally a matter of arbitrary judgement by the author. His translations of earthly failure into spiritual triumph certainly assert the rightness of remaining faithful to the promptings of the inner life and of rejecting the superficiality of the world's opinions. But the transformations remain to some extent improbable because the reader is given insufficient insight into the actual processes of spiritual growth and because the prose which is to vindicate the Christian paradox of the spirit incarnate in the flesh is often rhetorically assertive rather than exploratively convincing.

Riders in the Chariot combines a heroic grandeur of conception with a Gothic profusion of detail. The structure and detailed texture of the novel express an intense struggle to draw the whole of human existence into unity, the beautiful and the grotesque, the comic and the tragic. White's is an intensely moral and systematizing imagination. But the attempt to incorporate the more recalcitrant elements of modern life into a single system occasionally fails, because it taps a perverse strain in the author, as when Mrs Flack's eructations must be comically assimilated into the religious pattern as 'resurrections'. There is also a sense of strain and awkwardness in some passages in which the dwellers in Australian suburbia are transformed into biblical archetypes. Ultimately the interlocking profusion of mythic detail in *Riders in the Chariot* is more reminiscent of an unfinished jigsaw puzzle than the mystic unity of a sacred mosaic. It is the vision of duality that is wholly authentic, not the vision of harmony. In his social vision White is caught between a past he feels a need to disavow and a future he cannot espouse.

*

The concept of an ideal harmony reappears in *The Solid Mandala*, which, like so many of White's novels, is an extended metaphor. The idea of a circle, or even a child's marble, as a symbol of perfection is made explicit in the text when Arthur Brown consults an encylopaedia and with some difficulty spells out the definition he finds there.

> '*The Mandala is a symbol of totality. It is believed to be the "dwelling of the god". Its protective circle is a pattern of order super-imposed on – psychic – chaos. Sometimes its geometric form is seen as a vision (either waking or in dream) or –*'
> His voice had fallen to the most elaborate hush.
> '*Or danced*' Arthur read. (*SM*, p. 238)

This incident clarifies the meaning of the central symbol, but it does not include the idea of quaternity, the square within the circle. In Arthur's mystic dance before Mrs Poulter, the notion of quaternity is given bodily expression as he dances in the four corners, each corner associated with a person closely connected with him. Clearly, it is unnecessary to go outside the text to understand the significance of the mandala in Arthur's quest for wholeness, but some knowledge of Jung's writings is a help and we know that before White wrote this novel the painter Lawrence Daws gave him a copy of Jung's *Psychology and Alchemy*.

The centre of interest in *The Solid Mandala* is the contrast and conflict between the twin brothers, Arthur and Waldo Brown. They are twin consciousnesses, each imperfect in a contrary fashion. They are separate yet closely linked by birth and long association. We first see them as old men through Mrs Poulter's eyes and then the narrative unfolds their whole lives up to this point. They are two distinct but potentially complementary parts of a single whole. Arthur is the simple, selfless, loving brother; Waldo, with sterile pretensions to learning, is distorted by self-will and hatred. In *Flaws in the Glass*, White confesses that he sees the two Brown brothers 'as my two halves', and that 'Waldo is myself at my coldest and worst' (*FG*, pp. 146–7).

The ingenious fourfold structure of *The Solid Mandala* serves the novelist well in developing his major theme, the quest for wholeness. It consists of: a brief prologue, called 'In the Bus'; two long central sections, the first presenting the story mainly from Waldo's point of view and the second from Arthur's; and, finally, the terrible climax which combines the grotesque and the apocalyptic in a characteristic fashion – grotesque details of the dogs savaging Waldo's dead body and Arthur's apocalyptic vision of his union with the divine, symbolized in the orange disc of the sun, an image consistently associated with Arthur throughout the novel.

In the central sections, headed 'Waldo' and 'Arthur' respectively, by a narrative *tour de force*, White keeps in the forefront of our minds the image of the two old men and their dogs on their daily walk, while at the same time building up a vivid sense of interconnecting scenes from their past and the past lives of the other characters, especially Mrs Poulter, through whose eyes we first see the two men and who finally bestows on Arthur the status of 'a modern saint'. Life is traditionally pictured as a journey. On this last walk, the different stages in Arthur's and Waldo's living journey appear before the reader's eyes. What gives each incident its importance is its function in the psychological and spiritual development of each character. We are primarily concerned with the inner life, as the epigraphs from Paul Eluard and Meister Eckhart remind us: Eluard's 'There is another world, but it is this one', and Eckhart's 'It is not outside, it is inside: wholly within.'

White's special gift for rendering inner and outer worlds simultaneously can be seen in a passage that contrasts the outsiders' view of the two brothers 'as frail and putrid' with the narrator's view and with their own view of themselves as they gaze at their own reflections.

> Gathered by the wind the two old men flitted across the plate glass, each examining himself, separately, secretly. On the whole each was pleased, for reflections are translatable symbols of the past . . . Arthur, for instance . . . was still able to enjoy the gusty light of boyhood in the main street of Sarsaparilla, his lips half open to release an expression he had not yet succeeded in perfecting. His body might topple, but only his body. The drier, the more cautious Waldo walked taking greater care in spite of the strength of his moral convictions. (*SM*, p. 55)

Unobtrusively the text reveals the core of reality beneath superficial appearance.

Yet though it is with the inner meaning of events that White is primarily concerned, he succeeds magnificently in giving colour, shape and form to the external action, maintaining a delicate balance between the personal psychology of the characters and archetypal patterns. Sufficient is revealed of the relationship of the twin boys to their parents to explain the formative influences on their contrasting psychological development. In this pattern, the deaths of the parents and the twins' relations with women play important parts. The contrasted reaction to the father's death dramatizes their radically different responses to experience. Waldo, who represses his emotions and avoids direct contact with painful reality, is actually the first to discover Mr Brown's death. He remains silent and retreats into arid, emotionless solitude in the garden. Arthur, on the other hand, touches his father (*SM*, p. 269) and gives immediate unselfconscious expression to his grief and

52

despair: 'He was bellowing. "Our father," he bellowed, "our father is *dead*!"' (p. 71).

The twin brothers are also defined in their relations to women: to Dulcie Feinstein, whom they both love, and Mrs Poulter. It is typical of Waldo's self-centred single-mindedness that Dulcie's engagement to Leonard Saporta should come as a surprise. When he arrives to propose to Dulcie himself, he is amazed to find Arthur there beside her. Waldo's calculating materialism and destructive energy are both clear when he walks over to Dulcie's house on this occasion: 'As he walked along the roadside, thoughtfully decapitating the weeds, Waldo went over the way in which he would benefit by marriage to Dulcie' (p. 149). In complete contrast, Arthur establishes a loving relationship with Dulcie that is based on affection, sincerity and the capacity to enter into the feelings of another. His innocent friendship with Mrs Poulter is also contrasted with Waldo's obsessive suspicion of women.

The second section of the narrative, 'Waldo', ends with the librarian brother's discovery of a poem by Arthur, beginning 'My heart is bleeding for the Viviseckshunist', his burning of the poem, Arthur's apology, and Arthur's cry, 'Let me go! Wald! *Waldo*!' (p. 214). The ending picks up two dominant images in the novel: the mandala and the yellow marigold sun, both images of life and rounded completeness and both consistently connected with Arthur.

'That poem? That disgusting *blood* myth!' Waldo gasped to hear his own voice.

'I would have given the mandala, but you didn't show you wanted it.'

'I never cared for marbles. My thumb could never control them.'

He was entranced by Arthur's great marigold of a face beginning to open.

Opening. Coming apart. Falling.

'Let me go! Wald! *Waldo*!'

As dropping. Down. Down. (pp. 213–14)

The full meaning of this does not become apparent until the end of the third section, called 'Arthur', which ends with a different view of the same scene. By that time, we have seen many of the incidents from Arthur's angle, or rather with the sympathetic emphasis falling on him. From the later view of the confrontation between the twin brothers, it is clear that Arthur's poem seemed obscene because it revealed a truth about femininity and suffering that Waldo could not assimilate. Waldo's reaction reveals his hatred of life. Arthur now sees the 'hatred Waldo was directing, had always directed, at all human beings, whether Dulcie Feinstein, or Mrs Poulter, or the blasphemous poem – because that, too, had life of a kind – the poem which celebrated their common pain' (p. 294). This recognition scene that White has staged with such theatrical finesse, withholding information at the end of the 'Waldo' section and releasing it at the end of the 'Arthur' section, reveals that Waldo dies recognizing for the first time the mutual dependence of the twin brothers, but unable to profit by the insight, and actually willing Arthur's death. Arthur, in an excess of simple magnanimity, takes on himself the whole responsibility for Waldo's hatred, thus demonstrating his understanding of the reciprocal and interacting forces of love and hatred, life and death.

The last framing action brings the novel into final focus, although some of the grotesqueries may seem gratuitous. Just as a worldly conversation in *Riders in the Chariot* asserts that Mrs Godbold is 'a modern saint', so Arthur's apotheosis is suggested through a snatch of dialogue between Mrs Poulter and Sergeant Foyle. '"This man would be my saint," she said, "if we could still believe in saints. Nowadays," she said, "we've only men to believe in. I believe in this man"' (*SM*, p. 314). Precisely. How well this points to White's dilemma as an artist. In a secular society he wants to write about saints and visionaries. Yet he also wants to assert their all too fallible nature, to affirm that the route to perfection lies through human fallibility. Some gap in credibility is almost inevitable.

The playfulness and literary quality of this novel, so acutely analysed by Brian Kiernan, sets both author and reader at a distance from the characters. The great variety of tonal shifts makes it extremely difficult to know how seriously to take many of the incidents.[13] For the committed Jungian critic, *The Solid Mandala* may well seem White's masterpiece, the novel in which his personal vision of life reaches a new depth and coherence as a result of being mediated through Jung's systematic schema. For the uncommitted critic, it must remain a highly problematic work, one in which there is a playful tension between myth and reality, symbol and concrete experience, tragedy and comedy, affirmation and doubt.

*

The same is not true of the extravagant and rebarbative novel that followed, *The Vivisector*, in which White commits himself to the anti-humanist implications of the artist as divinely inspired vivisector, one whose artistic calling justifies all manner of selfishness, cruelty and manipulation of others. In *Flaws in the Glass*, White says that the novel 'is about a painter, the one I was not destined to become – another of my frustrations' (*FG*, p. 150). There is another passage in the autobiography which is equally revealing about the identity felt between the novelist and his created artist, Hurtle Duffield. It begins by asking the question 'What do I believe?' and goes on to ask 'Am I a destroyer? this face in the glass which has spent a lifetime searching for what it believes, but can never prove to be, the truth. A face consumed by wondering whether truth can be the worst destroyer of all' (*FG*, p. 70).

The Vivisector attempts to demonstrate the necessary and reciprocal relations of destruction and creation. There are obvious advantages in the choice of an artist figure for developing a quasi-religious vision of God immanent in the world. The novel as a whole may be seen as a vast extension of the epigraph from the English abstract painter Ben Nicholson: 'As I see it painting and religious experience are the same thing and that what we are all searching for is the understanding of infinity.' Certainly when the artist Hurtle Duffield remarks, 'take an honest-to-God kitchen table, a kitchen chair, what could be more real', this occurrence of one of White's favourite images of bedrock reality seems very much more natural and authentic than the gnomic utterances about tables by the gross Will Lusty in *The Ham Funeral* or Stan Parker in *The Tree of Man*. But the most obvious faults in the total conception of the novel are Hurtle Duffield's inadequacy as either a Faustian figure or a cursed Romantic artist, the lack of any sustained, ironic scrutiny of the hero, who remains throughout a privileged visionary, and the excessively schematic nature of the whole. The schematization becomes far too overt in the last third of the novel. There, a series of letters, meetings and confessions is contrived to demonstrate that there is a kind of freemasonry of 'burnt ones': in the painfully deformed Rhoda's words, the idea that 'almost everyone carries a hump, not always visible, and not always of the same shape' (*Viv*, p. 469); or as Mrs Volkov reports Cutbush as saying, 'we was all perhaps *stroked by God*' (*Viv*, p. 613). The last excruciating pun on the word 'stroke' when Duffield is dying – which has delighted some critics – is typical of the rib-crushing obviousness of White's nudges in the direction of a theology that would reconcile human infirmity and divine providence. In view of the profusion of scatological imagery and the anti-humane theme, it is hardly surprising that in 1970 the Swedish Academy decided that it could not award a Nobel Prize to 'an author whose latest work elaborates on the not at all attractive conclusion that the artist steps over dead bodies in order to give free sway to life; that he consumes people as the raw material of his art'.[14]

4

PLAYS AND SHORT STORIES

From the age of 9 when he wrote his first play *The Mexican Bandits* White was stage struck. He forced his tomboy sister into family theatricals; and, during his public school holidays, he 'spent hours hanging round stage doors waiting for the stars to come out' (*FG*, p. 54). Later he moved in minor theatrical circles centred on the Arts Theatre Club in London. In 1933, two plays that have since disappeared were put on at Bryant's theatre in Sydney; and, in addition to contributing sketches to London revues, he had his play *Return to Abyssinia* put on briefly in 1946 at Bolton's experimental theatre in London. Then, between 1946 and 1948, he wrote *The Ham Funeral*, which had to wait for its first production until 1961 in Adelaide. There followed in fairly quick succession *The Season at Sarsaparilla* (1962), *A Cheery Soul* (1963) and *Night on a Bald Mountain* (1964); and in the late 1970s, there was another flurry of dramatic activity, marked by *Big Toys* (1977), *Signal Driver* (1982) and *Netherwood* (1983). The last of these, *Netherwood*, which was performed to packed houses, seemed to me as I watched it almost like an unconscious parody of White's favourite themes and paradoxes. In the final shoot-out between the 'insane' forces of social order and the 'sane' inhabitants of a private mental home, nearly the whole cast is shot dead, just as it was in his 9-year-old effort, *The Mexican Bandits* (*FG*, p. 26). The dramatic wheel has come full circle.

The plays are little known outside Australia but have probably encouraged younger Australian dramatists to continue their experiments with non-naturalistic forms, such as popular music-hall and vaudeville routines, and to use a much wider range of language. Several are highly successful dramatic pieces and all throw light on the main themes and style of the novels, especially the conflict between the masculine and feminine in the human psyche and the conflict between natural feeling and social conformity. All the plays owe a very general debt to European expressionism and are therefore not to be judged as realistic drama. But the problems of response and judgement are complex. The inclusion of realistic social satire and dialogue that so accurately mimics the different varieties of Australian speech makes it difficult to see the plays as examples of expressionist art, that is an art that makes no claim to represent social reality but which, through image, symbol and conscious distortion, releases the unconscious and transcends photographic realism. J. R. Dyce suggests that White 'has attempted to synthesize the poetic realism of Chekhov and Tennessee Williams and the psychoanalytic depth of Strindberg and O'Neill'.[15] One might also add a rather general debt to Ibsen, in that all the plays are symbolic expansions of a central metaphor embodied in their title.

White's highly developed theatrical sense is immediately apparent in the large-scale arrangement of the dramatic action. In *The Ham Funeral*, he sets the action vertically in a lodging house, as a visual representation of the divisions within the human psyche. Thematically, the play suggests the need for the idealistic Young Man upstairs to establish human relations with the gross figures of Mr and Mrs Lusty in the basement below. On the upper level of the playing space, the Young Man is involved in another process of conflict, the struggle towards individuation, which involves The Girl in the next room, whom he never sees. This part of the action, as White makes explicit in a programme note, dramatizes 'the dialogue between the Young Man and his anima' (*FP*, p. 3). He goes on to explain:

The Relatives become the expression of the conscience. . . .
As for the scavengers, a lapse of time and change of scene
were necessary, so I gave way to my weakness for music-hall.
In any case, many interludes are a mixture of the hilarious
and the brutal. (*FP*, p. 4)

The structure of the play as a whole suggests that only after
achieving some degree of psychic individuation can the young
man accept the earthly world embodied in the lives of Mr and
Mrs Lusty and confront life positively – more positively than
Elyot Standish, the hero of White's second novel, *The Living
and the Dead*.

In *The Season at Sarsaparilla*, the spatial arrangements are
primarily horizontal – not vertical as in *The Ham Funeral* –
although certainly the cellar where the children play, share their
dirty secrets, and where Pippy sees the dogs copulate, acts as an
important vertical division to express the distance between
subterranean instincts and social behaviour. White divides the
horizontal space into three segments, each comprising a back-
yard, a kitchen and a suggestion of a house behind. The stage
directions make it clear that it is an expressive set, not a
naturalistic one, and that there should be a minimum of
furniture and a good deal of miming. The tripartite division of
the stage is an ingenious device for presenting the patterns and
rhythms of life in the three families: the Knotts (stage right), the
Pogsons (centre) and the Boyles (stage left). Quick switches
from one playing area to another emphasize contrasts. The set
also provides for elaborate contrapuntal sequences that express antithetic responses to experience.

Since the stage set is simple, most of the ordinary actions
have to be mimed. Consequently the play develops a strong
ritualistic quality. This is central to White's vision. The set
dramatizes the extent to which the inhabitants of modern
suburbia are involved in three basic rhythms. Two of these are
man-made, the other is natural. The first consists of the dull,
sterile domestic rhythms enacted in the three kitchens, especially by the heavily pregnant Mavis Knott and the ultra-dainty

Girlie Pogson. The second is the mechanical 'in/out' rhythm imposed by the demands of meaningless work, a rhythm which is enormously speeded up at the end of the play by the razzle-dazzle of light and by Roy Child's choric commentary: 'So the men of Mildred Street continue on their way . . . out, in . . . in, out' (*FP*, p. 173). In contrast to these two suburban rituals, one domestic and the other industrial, are the altogether more natural rituals of the children playing and, related to these, the quite instinctive rituals of the dogs and the bitch (or as the dainty Girlie Pogson insists on calling it, 'the lady dog'). It is a minor fault of this play that the sounds of the dogs are so obtrusive and that the link between the bitch and Nola Boyle, the Australian Molly Bloom, is so naked and explicit. A similar insistence on the natural instincts of the goatkeeper, Miss Quodling, and her goats damages the expressive power of *Night on a Bald Mountain*. Symbols in drama work best when they are used sparingly (as the breaking string in Chekhov's *Cherry Orchard*), when their meaning is to some extent ambiguous (as in Ibsen's *The Master Builder*), and when the audience has to reach out imaginatively to realize their full significance.

The Season at Sarsaparilla is a fine piece of theatre that has been successfully revived in recent years. Undoubtedly its chief strength lies in the ingenuity and coherence of its dramatic structure and the enormous vitality of the language. Although the action, which effectively contrasts natural and artifical rhythms in suburban life, involves all three households, the real dramatic interest centres on Ernie and Nola Boyle. Nola, like many of White's flawed women, inhabits a different realm from the other women in the play; she is altogether more vibrant and alive, and her relationship with her limited but honest husband touches our deeper emotions as does nothing else in the play, certainly not the melodramatic death of Julia Sheen, nor the birth of Mavis's child, nor the reconciliation of Judy and her drab nonentity of a husband. Ultimately this causes an imbalance between the three playing areas on the stage, and John Burrows is probably right in saying that

White's intention in the play is 'betrayed by the startling tonal disparities between the cool sarcasm of the chorus and the intense passions that are enacted, above all in the history of the Boyles'.[16] The Nola and Ernie relationship is so much deeper and more dramatically moving than anything else in the play that it makes the rest seem thin and insubstantial.

Undoubtedly the successful revival of *The Season at Sarsaparilla* in 1976 reawakened White's interest in the theatre. The three plays that followed in quick succession are very different from each other. In the first, *Big Toys* (1977), White uses the artificial conventions of high comedy for a serious political purpose (as Louis Esson did back in 1912 in *The Time Is Not Yet Ripe*): he exposes the shallowness and moral irresponsibility of the 'Beautiful People' who rose to positions of power and influence in the late 1970s. The play presents a remarkably inclusive criticism of society but its methods are often unexpectedly oblique. For example, it only emerges late in the play and somewhat indirectly that uranium mining is the real issue over which the union leader Terry has compromised his integrity. Here the approach is in strong contrast with White's passionately direct condemnation of uranium mining in 'The Role of the Australian Citizen in a Nuclear War', a speech given at a Canberra symposium. The subtle inclusiveness and obliquity of approach in the play is not matched by the kind of fine wit and incisiveness essential to the success of high comedy. In the final showdown, when the compromised unionist Terry hands back the keys of the Ferrari, his rejection and exposure of the false values of the lawyer Ritchie and his beautiful parvenue wife Mag depend too much on the shock tactic in the stage direction and too little on the supporting dialogue, which is strained and literary. The stage direction reads: 'TERRY goes up to RITCHIE, pulls at his cheeks as if they had been rubber and plants a clumsy, smacking kiss on his open mouth.' In harmony with the play's title and recurrent imagery, however, Terry makes a speech prophesying that the explosion resulting from men-of-power's 'selecting their partners for the great uranium ball' will be 'the biggest, gaudiest toy that ever escaped from a child's hand' (*BT*, p. 56). Katherine Brisbane, in her Preface to the play, remarks: 'High Comedy – the art form of brilliance, superficiality, heartlessness and fierce social criticism – is the perfect form in which to express such a message', and clearly believes that White has reached such perfection. But the play seems to me only intermittently theatrical; the producer's footnotes are sufficient proof of the effort needed to translate the often rather literary and undramatic dialogue into significant dramatic action. The play also reinforces the truth that White has a well-developed sense of humour but no sense of the humourless.

The action of *Big Toys* takes places in winter and spring, whereas White's next play, *Signal Driver*, has the chronological expansiveness of his longer fiction. Within its brief three acts are compressed the main phases in the long marriage of Theo and Ivy Vokes which stretches from the First World War to the present. Perhaps encouraged by the 'New Wave' dramatists' serious use of music-hall routines, as in Jack Hibberd's superb monodrama *A Stretch of the Imagination*, White returns to the grotesque playfulness of the creatures rummaging through garbage cans in *The Ham Funeral*. He creates two Beings, one masculine, the other feminine, who clown, dance, sing and provide choric comments on the nature of love and death, idealism and practicality, illusion and reality, as these are illustrated in the lives of an ordinary, suburban couple. The initial stage direction shows how far White's paradoxical imagination is willing to go to stress the necessary connection between filth and illumination (compare *The Vivisector*), between the crudely grotesque and the elemental (compare the climax of 'The Night the Prowler'): 'They have rolled around so long on earth that the rags and bags they are wearing are coated with the thickest scunge. Their hair is matted with filth and lice, their faces are only just distinguishable' (*SD*, p. 5). Comparison with Beckett reveals how much in *Signal Driver* depends on actors and producer, for the dialogue and snatches of song are often threadbare and banal, consisting of an awkward blend of the knowing and the naïve. The play is redeemed by the moving and patently honest reconciliation of Theo and Ivy in decrepit old age. Then, Ivy who has never shared Theo's idealism and insight into ordinary reality, says simply: 'It's the table I love. Always there. Nothing like a table when it's a real one' (*SD*, p. 48). This favourite White trope works here, because it is supported by the earlier contrasts between Theo's devotion to his honest carpenter's craft and Ivy's meretricious success in selling phoney antiques, aided by her Jewish patron and lover. The last exchange between husband and wife is starkly tender: 'THEO: Rub yer shoulder for yer. . . . IVY: Glad to get in . . . shut everything out . . . (IVY and THEO disappear, supporting each other)'. In the first production, the play ended with a vast cloth, glowing with light, moving across the whole auditorium, 'the Aurora takes possession of the whole theatre'. This mystified the audience who had not read the stage direction. In the return season, only lighting was used to represent the aurora australis and the potential world of love that links all creation. Equally puzzling and ambiguous is the symbol embodied in the title *Signal Driver* and in the stage set. In each of the acts, Theo lifts a tentative hand to signal the tram or, later, bus, but they all pass by. Only an obtuse audience will reduce all this to a matter of 'missing the bus' in life. The dramatic action develops a rich and ambiguous set of meanings related to ambition, idealism and reconciliation to life's limiting circumstances.

*

The most obvious connection between White's work in the theatre and his fiction is the play *A Cheery Soul* (1963), originally written as a short story. Although it was much changed for the theatre, it already contained many of the characteristic elements of the later comic expressionist play. It is not surprising that Patrick White, the author of Australian epics and mammoth fictional psychodramas, should feel constrained by the limits of the short-story form. 'Short stories? I don't really like writing them much – All my effects are cumulative, and one doesn't really have time to get the effects you want.'[17] In spite of this statement, he has published two volumes of short stories, *The Burnt Ones* (1964) and *The Cockatoos* (1974). These stories have prompted varying critical responses, ranging from William Walsh's high praise of the story 'Down at the Dump' to the more negative judgement of John Burrows, who observes that they are 'damaged by the mechanical working out of a pre-ordained idea and by a unity of action that is contrived' rather than imagined. David Myers provides the most positive and illuminating account of these short stories, demonstrating how the controlling ironies establish a balance between the surface of social trivia and the hidden psychological and spiritual truths.[18]

Two characteristics of Patrick White's novels might suggest that he would have a problem in accommodating his expansive imagination to the limits of the short story. The first is the broad temporal span covered by the novels, the other is the process of narrative regression of which the hundred-page excursus into Theodora's past in *The Aunt's Story* is typical. In *The Burnt Ones*, the first story 'Dead Roses' and the last 'Down at the Dump' illustrate contrasting solutions to this narrative problem. In 'Dead Roses', White uses twenty numbered sections to relate the story of Anthea Scudamore's transformation into a replica of her conventional mother. The transformation occurs between her first visit to Kangaroo Island and her return many years later. Within this strictly chronological sequence there are a number of obvious devices to connect past and present, especially Anthea's widely separated confrontations with the virile Dr Flegg and the repeated image of the roses. In 'Down at the Dump', the handling of time is very different. This is a very Joycean story. The narrative, which ironically juxtaposes a funeral and a cheerful day's outing to a rubbish dump, uses stream-of-consciousness techniques to revive the spirit of the dead woman Daise Morrow. She has scandalized her family by her loving relations with various men, including the old dead-beat Ossie whom she revitalized in bed just before her death. 'Then the lad Ossie Coogan rode again down from the mountain, the sound of the snaffle in the blue air, the smell of sweat from under the saddle-cloth, towards the great, flowing river' (*BO*, p. 304). In the story the gap between the dead woman's censorious relatives and the feckless, cheerful Whalleys, who go down to the dump to give new life to discarded objects, is bridged by two members of the younger generation. Their shared dreams express the reality of love and forward-looking thoughts. This tale of a dead person and discarded rubbish consistently plays on the life/death paradox which is summed up in the dead woman's words, 'that death isn't death, unless it's the death of love' (*BO*, p. 311). 'Down at the Dump' possesses the concentrated force, the economy of means, the significant form and the crystallizing imagery that we associate with the short story at its best. It is not a telescoped novel as 'Dead Roses' is. Through its finely imagined form it expresses a complex vision of life.

White's different treatment of time and his choice of narrative method affects much else in these two very Australian stories, including their respective qualities as works of art. Like most of the other stories in *The Burnt Ones*, they contrast different responses to life. They contrast those who, though damaged by experience (the 'burnt ones'), remain spiritually alive and those who through force of convention and compromise are spiritually dead. However, the contrasts are less extreme than in the novels and there are, strictly speaking, no elect; no one wins through to a secular salvation.

Half the stories in *The Burnt Ones* are set in Australia, the rest in Greece. Both groups share similar thematic preoccupations, but in the Greek stories there is less temptation to fall back on easy and obvious Barry Humphries-type effects. Most critics have praised White's skill in creating his Greek characters, who are full of nervous energy, even when tamed by experience. They have also admired his vivid evocation of the odd mixture of wild passion and beauty with the tawdry and the trivial. With no scores to work off against hated suburbia the author's tone is more equable and controlled. Of the Greek stories, 'The Woman Who Wasn't Allowed to Keep Cats' is the best. Its excellence arises from the ironic contrasts developed between the two wealthy Americanized Greeks and their old friends, the Greek couple whom they visit in Athens. It also arises from the vivid rendering of the changing relationship between the cat-loving wife and her idle, Oblomov-like husband, who finally forbids her to keep any cats in the new flat. The coda describing the 'hour of gold, the radiant beauty of Greece', as the visiting couple leave for America, effectively signalizes their incapacity to respond to the passionate intensity of living that shocked them when the husband reports the wild love-making he witnessed through their friends' bedroom window. 'Some people are like animals', his wife protests, unable to reassess her own sterile relationship with her obtuse husband in the light of this revelation. In this story, as in many others, Greece becomes a symbol of the possibilities of redemption through beauty and intense passion, just as Italy was for E. M. Forster.

The second collection of short stories, *The Cockatoos* (1974), has as its explanatory subtitle *Shorter Novels and Stories*. The opening and closing novellas, 'A Woman's Hand' and 'The Cockatoos', illustrate how much more easily White moves within this ampler form, while the briefer 'The Night the Prowler' is a concentrated *tour de force* out of which White later created a successful film script. All three explore modern distortions of love. Since 'A Woman's Hand' is an ironic exposure of female manipulation, it is a pity that the heavy male hand of the narrator is so obvious. By means of a flashback to a compromising sexual encounter in Egypt after the First World War, it develops a familiar White contrast between the solitary male integrity of Clem Dowson and the uncomprehending manipulation of others by Evelyn Fazackerley and her reluctant and more sensitive husband Harold, who has been instinctively drawn to Clem since boyhood and is granted a vision of the unity of opposites, of 'fur and feather', too late in life for it to produce anything but a revelation of his deep hatred of his wife. The formerly complacent couple are inveterate travellers. The final irony, after their indirect responsibility for Clem's probable suicide and his wife's mental breakdown, is their decision to set off to visit 'the Dead Heart' of Australia (C, p. 86).

Altogether more violent and extreme in its contrast of natural feeling and repressive social norms is the grotesque story of the young girl Felicity Bannister, in 'The Night the Prowler'. She is granted her moment of illumination after her wild nocturnal raids on social propriety, when she shares a shelter with an old wino who dies holding her hand. In one of White's most improbable assertions of the coexistence of degradation and spiritual becoming, we are told that Felicity has come to know herself in the old derelict as well as in the 'dizzy course' of perpetual becoming (C, p. 154). No similar epiphany is granted to the characters in the densely textured and finely conceived story 'The Cockatoos'. Through consistently maintained ironic viewpoints, the reader is given various insights into the nature of true love and the symbolic significance of the cockatoos. In no other story does White combine so well the psychological curiosities of suburban life with illuminating symbolism. The details of the couple who have not spoken for years but have communicated by notes, and the details of the husband's nightly visits to the other woman for a plateful of overdone steak, are realized with all the sober authenticity we associate with V. S. Pritchett. The cockatoos that mysteriously sweep down on the couple's lawn and as mysteriously disappear suggest the mysteries of grace and transcendence in a much less obtrusive fashion than the symbols in the titles of such stories as 'Dead Roses' and 'A Woman's Hand'.

The plays and short stories are very much a piece with the novels. They share similar preoccupations with solitary vision, the duality of all things and the lonely quest for some reconciling harmony which is only to be achieved through suffering and painful immersion in the inadequacies of the physical world. They display extraordinary inventiveness of technique and an immensely courageous attempt to mix different modes and styles, and, in the case of the short stories, to provide ironic codas that make the natural climaxes of the stories highly problematic, so that the reader is made to reassess everything that has gone before.

5

LAST NOVELS: 'THE ORDINARY ONES'

Like *The Vivisector*, the next novel is a portrait of a city, the Sydney that Patrick White had known in his youth and came to know again when he moved down from Castle Hill, once rural, now part of raw suburbia, to Centennial Park, in the centre of the city. In *The Eye of the Storm* the main action focuses on the dying Elizabeth Hunter in her house at Centennial Park. Although her daughter Dorothy's conversation during an aeroplane flight with a Dutchman about the calm at the eye of the storm, and her son's and daughter's incestuous night in the family country home play an important part, they are subordinated to the scenes enacted around the death-bed of the once beautiful Sydney socialite, Elizabeth Hunter. It is a very theatrically conceived novel, beginning, as do many stage plays, just before the climax of the action. The vain, decayed socialite is a modern Cleopatra who has known how to bewitch men in the past and still retains a curious magnetism: 'age cannot wither her, nor custom stale her infinite variety.'[19] She assumes her stage masks each time Sister Flora Manhood brings her the vanity box. At the climax of the novel, the former cabaret star, Lottie, who is now Elizabeth's cook, dances a dance of life and death before her mistress, who dies as 'a ravaged queen on her throne' (*ES*, p. 442). Elizabeth's son, the actor Sir Basil Hunter, who has sped to her death-bed for materialistic motives, cannot make a move without considering its dramatic effect, even at the very moment of his reunion with his mother:

> On catching sight of the figure in the wheelchair, Sir Basil hesitated the tick of a second, as though he had found an understudy waiting on the spot where his leading lady should have been; then (your performance is what matters; curse the management only after the curtain calls) he continued across the carpet with that distinctive limp. (*ES*, p. 118)

The nurses thrill to 'the riches in the voice' when he greets his dying mother: 'Darling – what a homecoming!' (p. 118). One of the incidental sources of amusement is the consistency with which Sir Basil's actions are accompanied by actual stage directions.

Like many actors, Basil is inordinately vain, apt to transform ordinary experience into a continuing drama with himself as the hero and totally preoccupied with what his next major role will be. His choice lies between attempting to redeem his past failures in playing Lear or risking everything in playing a role that his friend Mitty Jacka has created in a fluid and amorphous drama. His – and all the other characters' – real problem is how to discover and fully realize the 'unplayed I'.[20] The idea comes from Mitty Jacka's note: 'an actor tends to ignore the part which fits him best *his life* Lear the old unplayable is in the end a safer bet than the unplayed I' (*ES*, p. 238). In various ways, most of the characters fail to realize their true selves because they lack the courage to play the unplayable I, which involves among other things a recognition of the continuity of past and present and uniting the light and dark sides of the self.

As the novel develops, it becomes clear that Elizabeth Hunter has made the mistake of trying to disavow and cancel the past. For instance, she tries to obliterate the reality of her adultery with the politician Athol Shreve and she has turned her back on the saving revelation that occurred on Brumby Island: she had seen in a 'bird impaled on a tree' a perfect image of suffering (p. 395) and had experienced 'a dream of glistening peace' at the centre of the cyclone, when 'all else was dissolved by this lustrous moment made visible in the eye of the storm' (pp. 409, 410). It is only on her death-bed that she interweaves past and present into a significant unity.

In memory old Mrs Hunter retraces her childhood act of drowning dolls in the river, her father's suicide, her adulteries, the late flowering of her love for her husband, and the potentially transfiguring experience on the island. Her present consists of the macabre last act of a dying queen or goddess, attended by two avaricious children and three benevolent spirits, or acolytes, Sisters Manhood, Badgery and de Santis. There is no death-bed repentance or reaffirmation of faith — no extreme unction as at the end of *Brideshead Revisited*. But there is a moment of transfiguring vision, when Elizabeth Hunter recognizes the illusory nature of physical reality and is caught up in the eternal world: 'Till I am no longer filling the void with mock substance; myself is this endlessness' (*ES*, p. 532). She achieves individuation by bringing together the dark and light sides of her self, but she also ensures her continuation in the lives of others through the gift of a turquoise necklace to Lal Wyburd, a dress to Lottie and a satin sash to Sister de Santis. It is typical of White's vision of the coexistence of the trivial and the sublime, the flesh and the spirit, that the transfiguration should occur when Mrs Hunter is seated on the commode (the Queen's 'throne'), and typical also that her death should coincide with the flow of Flora Manhood's menstrual blood, and, finally, typical too that Flora should see her dead mistress as slipping

> sideways on her throne while still hooked to the mahogany rails. One buttock, though withered, was made to shine like ivory where the rose brocade was rucked up. . . . Never had the nurse felt so powerless, so awkward, as in slewing this totem into its orthodox position. (*ES*, pp. 533–4)

There is an undoubted element of perversity in the whole conception. Yet it is an essential feature of White's vision that the extremes of the mundane and the other-worldly should intermingle and it could be argued that one of the strengths of the novel is that White never idealizes Elizabeth Hunter or minimizes the grotesque and humiliating aspects of senility and approaching death. Moreover, in considering Flora's image of the dying woman, it is important to see that each of the three nurses, apart from serving symbolic roles, typifies a different response to the old woman's death and the search for reality. At one extreme is Sister Badgery's cheerful philistinism while at the other is the devotion as a 'votary of life' of the saintly Mary de Santis, who is rewarded by participating in the joyful ritual of the birds on the last page of the novel. In between comes Flora Manhood, who serves Mrs Hunter with warm human devotion and looks unsuccessfully for happiness and fulfilment through her abortive relations with others: her brusque mate Col, her lesbian bus conductress cousin Snow, and Sir Basil, whose child she at first hopes to bear.

In direct contrast to old Mrs Hunter's humble achievement in coming to terms with her own past and recognizing the symbolic significance of the eye of the storm is the failure of her two children, Dorothy and Basil. At the end, Dorothy complacently congratulates herself on her escape. On the flight back to Europe she recalls in vulgar, worldly terms her previous plane companion's story of the eye of the storm and ridicules her mother's capacity for spiritual insight. 'And Mother what could Mother have told of her experience on Brumby Island? . . . could anything of a transcendental nature have illuminated a mind so sensual, mendacious, materialistic, superficial as Elizabeth Hunter's? (Poor Mummy! it is malignant to malign the dead)' (*ES*, p. 570). Dorothy's thoughts expose her own spiritual blindness, her lack of charity or insight into others. Basil's attempts to summon up remembrance of things past, however, show a genuine but desperately limited ability to connect the past with the present in order to discover the 'unplayed I'. Appropriately, the main set-piece is created in a comic-serious mode at the old family home of Kudjeri. Basil discovers his father's old 3-litre Bentley resting on flat tyres in the barn. Absurdly handicapped in his movements by the ill-fitting steel boot he has put on, Basil loses himself in an affectionate memory of the past, until his reverie is shattered by his sister's peremptory 'What are you doing?' He answers: 'Playing with this bomb. Don't you remember Dad's car?' (*ES*, p. 489). Dad – Alfred Hunter – is remembered by both old Mrs Hunter and her son as an embodiment of human goodness, but it is Basil's tragedy that, like so many of the novelist's male protagonists, he has never been able to establish warm human contact with his father. In this respect he mirrors his creator's relationship with his shy, reticent father, as indicated by the anecdote in *Flaws in the Glass* about the embarrassing facts of life lesson on a Swiss railway station and by the confession that if only there 'had been some vaguely intellectual ground' he would have loved his father, and that he would have loved him had they 'been able to talk to each other' (*FG*, pp. 14–15, 48).

For Dorothy and Basil the return to the past at Kudjeri fails to create either self-knowledge or any real contact with their parents as separate identities. It seems natural enough therefore that the regression to childhood should have as its climax the incestuous night in the parents' bed, the matrix of their own creation. In Jungian terms this incident symbolizes a victory for the Terrible Mother, a regression of the developing ego into undifferentiated nature; but this is certainly not part of White's design and there is something outrageously perverse about the whole conception of this scene.

One reaction to those who extol *The Eye of the Storm* as a modern *King Lear*, with Elizabeth Hunter at the still centre of the storm, is to insist that the real life of the novel lies in the comic portraiture, not in the over-schematic working out of the basic metaphor. The comic range is extremely wide. It ranges from low comedy at the bus conductress Snow's place to the high comedy of Flora Manhood's and Mary de Santis's parallel visits to Sir Basil's hotel room. Sir Basil himself is a masterpiece of comic portraiture. Throughout, White's eye for comic incongruity is superb. Two examples must suffice. The first is the description of the arrival of Dorothy – transformed by marriage into the Princesse de Lascabanes – at her mother's sick-bed.

> A Princess shouldn't run, the nurse recovered herself enough to disapprove, and she shouldn't have a horse face.
>
> But Dorothy floundered, imperviously, on. '*O mon Dieu, aidez moi!*' she gasped, before assuming another of her selves, or voices, to utter, 'Mother!' and lower, 'Mum!' (*ES*, p. 45)

How economically that exposes the incongruity between the Australian Dorothy Hunter and the returning Frenchified Princess. For an example of richer and deeper comic incongruities one can point to the old lady's dying moments with Lottie. Although Flora's comment, 'a couple of crazy bitches', is felt to be absolutely right in its context, it is not a judgement we endorse because we have been made to see the supreme value of Elizabeth's end.

Although the storm is a recurrent image, it is impossible to see Elizabeth as a female Lear, since she experiences no tragic agony as a result of filial ingratitude nor is she purged through tragic suffering. The free fictive life is sustained not so much by the chosen metaphor of the storm but by two other sources: the incongruous juxtaposition of opposites (the grotesque and the beautiful, the public and the private self, sympathy and selfishness, art and life); and secondly by the idea of the 'unplayed I', which touches major as well as minor characters, all of whom are struggling, however inadequately, to release the buried self.

*

The theme of the buried, secret self is central to the two novels that follow: *A Fringe of Leaves* (1976) and *The Twyborn Affair* (1979). In the first, the heroine Ellen, who is involved in the basic conflict between nature and culture that permeates the novel, struggles to realize her true identity. In the second the androgynous Eddie/Eadie struggles against family prejudice and social conventions to release 'the woman in man and the man in woman'. One novel assumes the outward form of a historical romance set in the Australian colonial past. The other is a psychological novel that spans the period from just before the First World War to the outbreak of the Second World War.

A Fringe of Leaves is Patrick White's most carefully composed and classically restrained novel. This is surprising since it includes scenes of cruelty and cannibalism, adultery and shipwreck, nakedness and savagery. The essential structure consists of a framing device made up of a social prologue in Sydney and a social epilogue at Moreton Bay, both couched in ironically civilized tones reminiscent of Jane Austen. Within this frame are two journeys: the sea voyage on the *Bristol Maid* before it is shipwrecked, and the heroine's hazardous land journey with the Aborigines and the escaped convict Jack Chance, who comes straight out of the pages of Mayhew's *London Life and the Labouring Poor*. On such journeys it seems natural for the various characters, especially Ellen Roxburgh and Jack Chance, to return in memory to earlier phases of their lives. Thus, at psychologically apt moments, the past is made to illuminate the present. A resemblance noted by Ellen between the Captain of the *Bristol Maid* and her farmer father brings back memories of a mystic vision at St Hya's Well and of how the scholarly, delicate Austin Roxburgh came to the Cornish farm to convalesce, and how after her parents' death he married her and initiated her into polite Cheltenham society.

The idea of initiation is an important one. This can be seen in White's treatment of Ellen's move from the rough and primitive Cornish farm to the sedate comfort of Birdlip Hill. The transition from 'simple farm girl who speaks Cornish dialect' to wealthy society lady who speaks received English is brought about by old Mrs Roxburgh. She initiates Ellen into the mysteries of civilized society. This involves the correct handling of teacups and keeping a literary diary of her daily activities. As Ellen comes to realize much later when she has been initiated into the primitive customs of the Aborigines, entry into polite society made her forget the essential truth that food 'is after all, life'. This truth, which she learnt on the primitive Cornish farm, faded 'while sipping chocolate . . . at Birdlip House, Cheltenham'. Her Cornish dialect faded also, only to resurface at significant moments when her authentic self breaks through the acquired social façade.

Without oversimplifying the novel, it is possible to see Ellen's quest for love and fulfilment as a journey which involves a series of initiations and trials, in each of which a figure introduces the passive heroine into another pattern or ritual of behaviour where she is tested. These other figures are: old Mrs Roxburgh; the amoral sensualist Garnet Roxburgh, Austin's brother; the Aboriginal family with whom Ellen lives; Jack Chance, the escaped convict; and finally, the respectable merchant widower, Mr Jevons. All these initiations and studied contrasts between different ways of life serve to develop the main theme of the novel, which is embodied in the title, *A Fringe of Leaves*. The novel as a whole portrays civilization as only a narrow fringe that disguises natural, more elemental forces beneath. The historical romance form becomes a vehicle for contrasting two ways of life and two value systems: we can call these the natural and the artificial, or the savage and the civilized, or nature and culture, or, using Lévi-Strauss's terms, the raw and the cooked. And the novel presents two basic variants of the natural: the first is Ellen's childhood in remote Cornwall, which was originally Celtic and which she thinks of as quite separate from the foreign civilization of England; and the second is her life among the Aborigines. The novel presents the artificial, civilized ways both sympathetically and ironically in a variety of guises: at the Roxburgh home at Birdlip; in Austin Roxburgh's clinging to Virgil's *Georgics* (even during the shipwreck) and his reduction of death to a mere literary conceit; and, more generally and ironically, in the precarious colonial culture in Australia in the 1830s, based on military force, brutal repression, convict labour and strained social etiquette.

After the shipwreck, after Ellen's participation in cannibal rites with the Aborigines, and after her initiation into the life of instinctive passion with Jack Chance, she returns to society: a return from nature to culture that is formally but subtly signalled when she crosses the dividing line between untamed bush and the tended plants of the Oakes's farm. The subsequent scene when the Commandant questions Ellen on all that has happened so that he can prepare his official report ironically dramatizes the contrast between reality (which the reader has lived through in the central sections of the novel) and society's version of reality, which is always and necessarily a polite fiction, a distortion of the truth for the purposes of maintaining social order. Colonial society, based on the rigid application of reason and law to all spheres of life, cannot admit mystery. To the Commandant's persistent questions about the secret ceremony she witnessed (which was the ritual eating of human flesh), Ellen replies guardedly:

> 'It was too private. For me too, I realized later. A kind of communion.'
> 'If it made such an impression on you, I should have thought you'd be able to describe it.'
> 'Oh, no!' She lowered the eyes she had raised for an instant in exaltation.
> The commandant threw down his quill, and sat back so abruptly the chair and his heels grated on the threadbare carpet. (*FL*, p. 329)

Critics who have condemned White for his supposed glorification of cannibalism, in effect align themselves with the obtuse, persistent Commandant. Although Ellen certainly sees the lives of the Aborigines as nasty and brutish, she finds a freedom and joy among them that she lacked in the stultifying social circles at Cheltenham with Austin. The cannibalism for Ellen is a sacramental feast, a communion with the divine.[21]

A Fringe of Leaves is the closest that Patrick White has come to providing a conventional happy ending. After many extraordinary adventures Ellen Roxburgh – one of the 'ordinary ones' – is reintegrated into society. As so often happens in White's novels, children play an important part in the final affirmation. In the child Kate, who is carrying 'the corpse of a fluffy chick',

Ellen sees an image of her former self, thus reconciling past and present, innocence and experience; and the circle of lively Lovell children represents one of the positive and creative aspects of the society to which she has returned. Nor are the children sentimentalized, as the references to the sly exchanges of kicks and punches make clear. Even if Ellen's donning of the smouldering garnet-silk dress seems to suggest too perfect a union of Garnet Roxburgh's passion and Austin Roxburgh's fidelity, the novel ends on a distinctly muted, qualified note, in the spinster Miss Scrimshaw's words: 'However much crypto-eagles aspire to soar, and do in fact, through thoughtscape and dream, their human nature cannot but grasp at any circum-stantial straw which may indicate an ordered universe' (*FL*, p. 366).

This is a very different vision from Wallace Stevens's 'Blessed rage for order', which is a purely aesthetic ideal. *A Fringe of Leaves* is White's most humanly convincing picture of the processes by which fallible human beings create little worlds of love and order from the most unlikely material. The novel also suggests the interdependence of the individual and the social psyche: it suggests that in the quest for wholeness and fulfil-ment, the individual must pass through the historic phases that have transformed savage tribes into civilized nations. We carry within us not only our own pasts but the past of the race. Neither must be denied. It is White's great achievement to have created a set of characters and events to embody this truth while at the same time preserving psychological credibility.

*

The Twyborn Affair is an equally positive and compassionate novel. Where earlier the themes of homosexuality and trans-vestism are touched on only incidentally and somewhat awkwardly, in *The Twyborn Affair* they become central for the first time. To say this is obvious but perhaps misleading. What is central is the search for personal identity; and to introduce such terms as homosexuality and transvestism is to impose society's defensive categories on what is essentially a psychic quest. In view of the prominence given to the artist figure earlier, it is surprising to find that this hazardous quester is not an artist but, instead, in the first phase the youthful mistress of an eccentric old Greek, in the second a vigorous jackeroo, and in the third the elegant madam of a fashionable London brothel. Once again we see the attraction of the impossible choice for White.

The narrative is so constructed that even the most perceptive reader will not penetrate the external disguise of the protagonist immediately but will be actively engaged in discovering the identity beneath the assumed persona. This is particularly true of the opening of the third phase when few clues are given at first to the identity of the brothel keeper, Mrs Trist. We are often almost as much in the dark as is the wealthy Joanie Golson at the beginning of the action when she gazes at the elderly Greek man and the 'charming young woman (daughter, ward, wife, mistress – whatever) leading her companion through the rambling maze' (*TA*, p. 12). She does not recognize in the young woman Eudoxia the son of her adored, very masculine Australian friend, Mrs Twyborn, although the letter that closes part 1 indicates that she believes she may have penetrated Eudoxia's disguise, and Mrs Golson pops up in each part of the novel as a potential threat to uncover the protagonist's identity.

The relationship between Eudoxia and Angelos turns on Eudoxia's irrational passion for the elderly Greek and a craving for the exotic and the ambiguous. It also turns on the polarities of attraction and repulsion. The opening pages of *A Fringe of Leaves* contain a passage that plays on this ambivalence, 'rocked together and apart'; in *The Twyborn Affair*, a description of the couple playing a four-hand piece at the piano makes the same point: 'The Vatatzes were playing, like many marriages, together and apart' (*TA*, p. 91). As Mrs Golson watches them, the tempo becomes more reckless and moves towards some physical crisis. She is reminded of her dying father's reproof of her own action 'in dancing at the Australia with a woman . . . in a corked-on moustache'. Since the woman

79

with the corked-on moustache was the protagonist's mother, the reflection establishes an ironic parallel between the bizarre couple at the piano and the respectable Mrs Golson's ambiguous relationship with Mrs Twyborn.

The transition from Europe to Australia is made by means of a shipboard sequence. The reader now meets the protagonist as the young wartime hero Eddie Twyborn, DSO, who is under no illusion about either human courage or his military award, but knows that 'courage is often despair running in the right direction' (*TA*, p. 120). Though dressed as a man, Eddie's sense of identity is still uncertain and ambiguous. At the ball on shipboard he finally runs away to his bunk to escape 'Mary's vulva' and the 'Colonel's crotch', each a source of distress and embarrassment. Throughout the novel great play is made on the idea of dressing up. There is the repeated suggestion that all professions engage in an elaborate ritual of dressing up to maintain the social self. Thus, in the shipboard sequence, military uniforms are seen as another form of dressing up, just as later Judge Twyborn's legal uniform with its high heels and black silk stockings is described with ambiguous sexual overtones. Finally, the expensive London brothel provides a further variation on the theme of nakedness and clothing, the private and the public self.

Eddie's return to his parents' house in Melbourne dramatizes his ambiguous relations with his mother and father. The reunion is an embarrassment all round. But two very important facts emerge. The first is Eddie's recognition that his mannish, dog-loving mother was 'himself in disguise', and that in some sense Angelos's doggy devotion was a substitute for his favourite dog Ruffles. The second is his recognition that his most intense emotional experiences had come from his father. One of these, a night spent in the same bed while travelling with his father, a judge, who was on circuit, clearly has incestuous implications and is frequently alluded to later in the narrative. When Mrs Trist spends a night at Lord Gravenor's, his confession that he liked to stroke his Nanny's moustache reminds the reader of the protagonist's loving encounter with his father's moustache, an image of the unity of masculine and feminine that continues to elude the questing protagonist.

In the central section of the novel dealing with Eddie's life as a jackeroo on a country property, White creates a marvellously wide variety of social types. These range from the station owner's sexually demanding wife Marcia Lushington to the simple-minded rabbit catcher Denny Allen and include the lively and compassionate portrait of the blowsy housekeeper Mrs Tyrell and the wholly convincing picture of the farm manager, Prowse. Don Prowse is a clergyman's son who has been deserted by his wife, has adopted rough outback habits but is sensitive underneath, and – like Eddie – is still in search of his sexual identity. Eddie oscillates between Marcia and Prowse. The climactic stages in Eddie's relationship with Prowse are well prepared. There is Eddie's baptismal immersion in water, accompanied by Prowse's jocular threats about buggery when he sees him naked. There is the detail of Eddie donning Marcia's clothing before Prowse's homosexual attack. When active and passive roles are reversed to satisfy Prowse's feelings of guilt, Eddie suddenly recognizes that 'Prowse's sighs of entreaty, his redundancies of love, were surprisingly like Marcia's' (*TA*, p. 259). This whole central sequence at Lushington's farm illustrates Eddie's failure to find fulfilment and true sexual identity with either a woman or a man. Disgusted and disappointed, he decides to leave immediately, and when we meet him next as Mrs Trist, keeper of a fashionable London brothel, he/she has decided never to dabble in sex again, except vicariously through his/her girls and their upper-class clients. But the experience at Lushington's in Australia has not been entirely negative. In Denny Allen's love for the child that had been incestuously fathered by another and in his loving fidelity to the shrewish Dot, Eddie has seen an image of transcendence. 'Happiness was perhaps the reward of those who cultivate illusion, or who, like Denny Allen, have it thrust upon them by some tutelary being, and then are granted sufficient innocent grace to sustain it' (*TA*, p. 217).

The scenes centred on the London brothel have a Firbankian

81

excess. But amid all the rich profusion of detail on the whores and their clients, their methods of satisfying each other, the bloody abortion of one, the death in action of Brigadier Blenkinsop on top of the negro Julie, certain structural elements stand out. For instance, there is an obvious contrast between the honest masquerades and illusions enjoyed at Mrs Trist's brothel and the dishonest and inauthentic behaviour at the country house significantly called 'Wardrobes', where Mrs Trist realizes that 'her every attempt at love had been a failure' and where in dreams she returns to her male identity, Eddie. Awakening, she reflects that 'War, death, and sex were the missing elements in this protected room.' In contrast to 'Wardrobes', what her London establishment possesses is natural innocence (she refers to her 'vernal nuns'), great vivacity, common honesty, simple relish in food, drink and sex. It is 'a world of fragmentation and despair in which even the perversities of vice can offer regeneration of a kind' (*TA*, p. 369). The brothel achieves reality by accepting the necessity of illusion – a more profound replaying of one of the master themes of *The Aunt's Story*.

In fact, there are three minor resolutions to the protagonist's quest. The first comes when Mrs Trist takes Gravenor's nephew Philip and initiates him sexually. This symbolic act of love and compassion unites Mrs Trist with her *alter ego*, Philip:

> The tremulous mirror he was offering her must have reflected the sympathy she felt for this boy. More than that: they were shown standing together at the end of a long corridor or hall of mirrors, which memory becomes, and in which they were betrayed stereoscopically, refracted, duplicated, melted into the one image, and by moments shamefully distorted into lepers or Velasquez dwarfs. (*TA*, p. 351)

The second resolution is marked by the climax of Mrs Trist's relations with Gravenor when we see that beneath his confident masculinity there lies a sexual ambiguity analogous to hers. The third and most important occurs when mother and son meet on the Embankment and through scribbled words on a prayer book the mother comes to accept her son's new identity: 'I've always wanted a daughter' (*TA*, p. 371). Following the mother's later suggestion that they should return to Australia together, they both cherish the unlikely prospect of a shared life. But everything in the scene suggests that such a conventional happy ending is impossible. Mrs Trist decides to hand over the brothel to the capable Ada and accepts the changed world conditions. 'My frivolous self will now go in search of some occupation in keeping with the times' (*TA*, p. 375), that is, accept the challenge of the Second World War. Wearing a cheap suit and a shirt a size too small, but still with female make-up on, Eddie goes to say goodbye to his mother. He never arrives; he is killed in an air raid and the novel ends with his mother cherishing a vision of the two drying their hair in the garden together: 'this fragment of my self which I lost is now returned where it belongs' (*TA*, p. 379). A Jungian might say that the return to the Terrible Mother must necessarily end in death.

It is completely in line with Patrick White's earlier fiction that parent and child, two fragments of a perfect whole, should experience their moments of vision at the point of expiration, real or figurative. It is also in line with his other work that most of the characters and human relationships should be part of a larger symbolic pattern, representing variations on the protagonist's quest for wholeness and identity. What makes this a particularly disturbing and enigmatic novel is that so many of the relationships are implicitly, if not explicitly, incestuous. From one point of view the moving reunion of mother and child on the Embankment is the compassionate resolution of a lifelong conflict and misunderstanding, but from another point of view it might be seen as marking the climax of infantile regression; in Freudian terms, a return to the womb, in Jungian terms, a final deathly surrender to the Terrible Mother. Such psychological simplifications, however, fail to do justice to the complexity of the work and the integrity of the artist.

From this puzzling but powerful novel three positives emerge, apart from the possibilities for harmony suggested by the Embankment reunion. The first and perhaps the least convincing comes from the value placed on Denny Allen's capacity to transform a cruel trick into a triumph of love. The second is the value placed on friendship – a kind of indirect tribute to White's forty-year friendship with Manoly Lascaris. And the third is the importance of recognizing 'the woman in man and the man in woman'. Coming from another writer, this emphasis on the androgynous might seem like an attempt to climb on a fashionable bandwagon; coming from Patrick White, it seems a humanistic solution to a problem that lies at the heart of all his fiction and – as we now know from the publication of *Flaws in the Glass* – his own life.

6

CONCLUSION:
WHITE AND THE CRITICS

It is not unusual for a highly original artist to be undervalued or misunderstood by his contemporaries. But in fact, Patrick White's works have been highly praised from the start, both in Australia and overseas:[22] yet the novelist himself has perpetuated the myth of misunderstanding and neglect. Why should this be?

It is, I suggest, a necessary stance, in line with White's championing of the despised and defeated in his novels. He identifies so closely with the Romantic tradition of the lone visionary that critics, academics and the general public are necessarily seen as hostile and uncomprehending. Such an attitude is actually inscribed in the texts of his novels, in the fate of Alf Dubbo's apocalyptic paintings and in the critics' hostility to Hurtle Duffield's disturbing art. The novelist's outbursts against critics and academics have become more, not less, intemperate with the passage of time. This is a situation to understand rather than deplore. As a non-cerebral writer who has always drawn deeply on the unconscious, White has a natural antipathy towards those who intellectualize art; and inevitably the volume of academic criticism has sharply increased with his growing fame. Like many writers he is particularly sensitive to tactless enquiries about work in progress. His antipathy to the academic process of canonizing texts is neatly illustrated by his disparaging remarks about *Voss* now that it has been canonized and made the subject of repeated academic analysis. He sees very clearly that the heavy hand of academicism not only destroys the life of the text but substitutes something altogether safer and less challenging. Yet he retains a passionate belief in the power of books to change the world and believes that his best books are *The Aunt's Story*, *The Solid Mandala* and *The Twyborn Affair* (FG, p. 145).

Amid all the diversity of critical opinion about White's work it is possible to isolate some of the more important strands. By stressing the combination of moral passion and intense imaginative power in White, liberal humanists like William Walsh have had little difficulty in placing his works within the English 'Great Tradition'. This is seen by others as inappropriate and limiting, as it does little justice to all the non-realistic elements in his fiction; it would be better, they suggest, to class him with such great American writers as Hawthorne or Melville, or the Russian novelist Dostoevsky. A third school of criticism insists that Patrick White has created a fictional genre of his own and that the works must be judged on their own terms and without relation to other forms and traditions. A more hard-headed and sceptical group, typified by Leonie Kramer, has concentrated on what is seen as a gap between intention and achievement in White, and has argued that very frequently the detailed texture of the work generates meanings that run counter to the overt intention embodied in the grand archetypal structure.

White's relations with his readers are as uneasy as those with his critics. In spite of his statement that he writes only for himself and has 'never thought about readership',[23] the texts presuppose and to some extent create two kinds of reader, the one literal-minded and obtuse, needing to be bullied, prodded and cajoled into seeing all the links in the grand design, the other intelligent, sensitive and imaginative, able to grasp the deeper significances of the text. This enormously complicates the reading process. Only in the perfectly modulated *The Aunt's Story* does White combine extreme originality with a relaxed confidence in his reader's sensitivity. In the works written after his return to Australia in 1948, the awkward tonal shifts create a sense of strain. This loss of confidence is understandable when it is remembered that his attempts to create a prose to 'convey a splendour, a translucence' in *The Tree of Man* were described by a leading poet and critic, A. D. Hope, as 'pretentious verbal sludge'. Allied to this loss of confidence was his growing disenchantment with Australian culture and suburban life. It is not surprising if at times the reader seems to be equated with the obtuse denizens of Sarsaparilla.

White's adversary type of art is inimical to orthodox criticism and to the established social order. Presumably it was the socially subversive elements as well as the visionary ones that first attracted him to European expressionism and surrealism. His own art, which has almost nothing in common with recent post-modernist fiction, has developed its own expressionist and surrealist techniques to explore the quest for truth in a grossly materialistic society. The early works chart the unresolved tensions between the individual and society as the characters pursue the paths of solitude, isolation and individual vision; the middle novels celebrate the powers of the privileged artist to reach truth – and White is quite dogmatic in saying 'I think the artist is privileged';[24] the last three novels suggest that some kind of reintegration into society is possible for the lonely spiritually elect. This new vision of a potential reconciliation between the alienated individual and social groups is accompanied by an altogether more compassionate view of human nature. White has finally reaped the rewards of his uncompromising honesty and integrity as an artist and a man.

NOTES

1 'Patrick White Interview: 9 December 1973', by Rodney Wetherell, Sunday Night Radio 2, Australian Broadcasting Commission.
2 T. Herring and G. A. Wilkes, 'A Conversation with Patrick White', *Southerly*, 33, 2 (1973), p. 139.
3 John Colmer, 'Duality in Patrick White', in R. Shepherd and K. Singh (eds), *Patrick White: A Critical Symposium* (Adelaide: The Flinders University of South Australia, 1978), pp. 70–6.
4 For a religious archetypal approach see Patricia A. Morley, *The Mystery of Unity: Theme and Technique in the Novels of Patrick White* (St Lucia, Qld: Queensland University Press, 1972); for a psychological and generic approach see Manfred Mackenzie's articles listed in the bibliography.
5 Herring and Wilkes, op. cit., p. 136.
6 Manfred Mackenzie, 'Patrick White's Later Novels', *Southern Review: An Australian Journal of Literary Studies*, 1, 3 (1965), p. 7.
7 Biographical details in this paragraph come mainly from White's essay 'The Prodigal Son', first published in *Australian Letters*, 1, 3 (April 1958), pp. 37–40, repr. in G. Dutton and M. Harris (eds), *The Vital Decade* (Melbourne: Sun Books, 1968), pp. 153–8; but see also other interviews listed in the bibliography.
8 Ibid., p. 157.
9 The essays by James McAuley and G. A. Wilkes are reprinted in G. A. Wilkes (ed.), *Ten Essays on Patrick White* (Sydney: Angus and Robertson, 1970), pp. 21–33, 34–46.
10 John Burrows, '*Voss* and the Explorers', *AUMLA*, 26 (November 1966), p. 234.
11 William Walsh, *Patrick White: 'Voss'* (London: Edward Arnold, 1976), p. 41.

12 'Patrick White', in Craig McGregor, *In the Making* (Melbourne: Nelson, 1969), p. 218.

13 Brian Kiernan, *Patrick White* (London: Macmillan, 1980), pp. 100–1.

14 Ingmar Björkstén, *Patrick White: A General Introduction*, trans. Stanley Gerson (St Lucia, Qld: Queensland University Press, 1976), p. 92.

15 J. R. Dyce, *Patrick White as Playwright* (St Lucia, Qld: Queensland University Press, 1974), p. 20; see also Peter Fitzpatrick, *After the Doll* (Melbourne: Edward Arnold, 1979), pp. 49–68.

16 J. F. Burrows, 'Patrick White's Four Plays', *Australian Literary Studies*, 2 (1966), pp. 155–70.

17 McGregor, op. cit., p. 220.

18 See William Walsh, *Patrick White's Fiction* (Sydney: Allen & Unwin, 1977), pp. 72–5; John Burrows, 'The Short Stories of Patrick White', *Southerly*, 24, 2 (1964), pp. 116–25, repr. in Wilkes (ed.), op. cit., pp. 163–81; David Myers, *The Peacocks and The Bourgeoisie: Patrick White's Shorter Fiction* (Adelaide: Adelaide Unversity Union Press, 1978).

19 Dorothy Green, 'Queen Lear or Cleopatra Rediviva? Patrick White's *The Eye of the Storm*', *Meanjin Quarterly*, 32 (December 1973), pp. 395–405.

20 Leonie Kramer, 'Patrick White: "The Unplayed I"', *Quadrant*, 18 (1979), pp. 65–8.

21 Don Anderson, 'A Severed Leg: Anthropophagy and Communion in White's Fiction', *Southerly*, 40 (1980), pp. 399–417.

22 See Alan Lawson's two densely documented essays on White criticism: *Meanjin Quarterly*, 32 (December 1973), pp. 379–91; *Texas Studies in Literature and Language*, 21, 2 (Summer 1979), pp. 280–95.

23 'Patrick White Interview', op. cit.

24 Ibid.

BIBLIOGRAPHY

WORKS BY PATRICK WHITE

Novels

The Immigrants. Unpublished, 1929–31.
Finding Heaven. Unpublished, 1929–31.
The Sullen Moon. Unpublished, 1929–31.
Happy Valley. London: Harrap, 1939. New York: Viking Press, 1939.
The Living and the Dead. London: Routledge, 1941. New York: Viking Press, 1941. Toronto: Macmillan, 1941.
The Aunt's Story. London: Routledge & Kegan Paul, 1948. New York: Viking Press, 1948. Toronto: Macmillan, 1948.
The Tree of Man. New York: Viking Press, 1955. Toronto: Macmillan, 1955. London: Eyre & Spottiswoode, 1956.
Voss. London: Eyre & Spottiswoode, 1957. New York: Viking Press, 1957. Toronto: Macmillan, 1957.
Riders in the Chariot. London: Eyre & Spottiswoode, 1961. New York: Viking Press, 1961.
The Solid Mandala. London: Eyre & Spottiswoode, 1966. New York: Viking Press, 1966.
The Vivisector. London: Cape, 1970. New York: Viking Press, 1970.
The Eye of the Storm. London: Cape, 1973. New York: Viking Press, 1974.
A Fringe of Leaves. London: Cape, 1976. New York: Viking Press, 1977.
The Twyborn Affair. London: Cape, 1979. New York: Viking Press, 1979.

Poetry

Thirteen Poems. Unpublished, n.d. [1929 or 1930].
The Ploughman and Other Poems. Sydney: The Beacon Press, 1935.

Plays

The Mexican Bandits. Unpublished, 1921.
Four Plays. (*The Ham Funeral, The Season at Sarsaparilla, A Cheery Soul, Night on a Bald Mountain.*) London: Eyre & Spottiswoode, 1965. Melbourne: Sun Books, 1967.
Big Toys. Sydney: Currency Press, 1978.
Signal Driver: A Morality Play for the Times. Sydney: Currency Press, 1983.
Netherwood. Sydney: Currency Press, 1983.

Film

The Night the Prowler. Directed by Jim Sharman, based on White's short story from the collection *The Cockatoos* (1974), 1979.

Short stories

'The Twitching Colonel'. *The London Mercury*, 35 (1937), pp. 602–9.
'Cocotte'. *Horizon*, 1 (1940), pp. 364–6.
The Burnt Ones. London: Eyre & Spottiswoode, 1964. New York: Viking, 1964.
The Cockatoos: Shorter Novels and Stories. London: Cape, 1974. New York: Viking Press, 1974.

Autobiography

Flaws in the Glass: A Self-Portrait. London: Cape, 1981.

Selected essays and speeches

'The Prodigal Son'. *Australian Letters* 1, 3 (1958), pp. 37–40. Repr. in G. Dutton and M. Harris (eds), *The Vital Decade*, pp. 153–8. Melbourne: Sun Books, 1968.
'Patrick White Speaks on Factual Writing and Fiction'. *Australian Literary Studies*, 10 (May 1981), pp. 99–101.
'The Role of the Australian Citizen in a Nuclear War'. In Robyn Williams (ed.), *The Best of the Science Show*, pp. 273–86. Mel-

bourne: Nelson and the Australian Broadcasting Commission, 1983.

BIBLIOGRAPHY

Australian Literary Studies publishes an annual bibliography of Patrick White in the May issue.

Beston, John B., and Beston, Rose Marie. 'A Brief Biography of Patrick White: A Note on the Dedications of Patrick White's Works: A Patrick White Bibliography'. *World Literature Written in English*, 12 (1972), pp. 208–29.

Finch, Janette. *Bibliography of Patrick White*. Adelaide: South Australian Libraries Board, 1966.

Lawson, Alan. *Patrick White*. Melbourne: Oxford University Press, 1974.

Scheick, William J. 'A Bibliography of Writings about Patrick White, 1972–78'. *Texas Studies in Literature and Language: A Journal of the Humanities* 21 (1979), pp. 296–303. (An issue devoted to the writings of Patrick White.)

SELECTED CRITICISM OF PATRICK WHITE

Books

Argyle, Barry. *Patrick White*. Edinburgh: Oliver & Boyd, 1967.

Beatson, Peter. *The Eye in the Mandala. Patrick White: A Vision of Man and God*. London: Elek, 1976. Sydney: Reed, 1977.

Berg, Mari-Ann. *Aspects of Time, Ageing and Old Age in the Novels of Patrick White, 1939–1979*. Gothenburg: University of Gothenburg, 1983.

Björkstén, Ingmar. *Patrick White: A General Introduction*, trans. Stanley Gerson. St Lucia, Qld: University of Queensland Press, 1976.

Brissenden, R. F. *Patrick White*. London: Longman, for the British Council and the National Book League, 1966.

Colmer, John. *Patrick White: 'Riders in the Chariot'*. Melbourne: Edward Arnold, 1978.

Dutton, Geoffrey. *Patrick White*. Melbourne: Lansdowne, 1961.

Dyce, J. R. *Patrick White as Playwright*. St Lucia, Qld: University of Queensland Press, 1974.

Kiernan, Brian. *Patrick White*. London: Macmillan, 1980.

McCulloch, A. M. *A Tragic Vision: The Novels of Patrick White*. St Lucia, Qld: University of Queensland Press, 1983.

Morley, Patricia A. *The Mystery of Unity: Theme and Technique in the Novels of Patrick White*. Toronto: McGill-Queen's University Press, 1972. St Lucia, Qld: University of Queensland Press, 1972.

Myers, David. *The Peacocks and the Bourgeoisie: Patrick White's Shorter Fiction*. Adelaide: Adelaide University Union Press, 1978.

Shepherd, R., and Singh, K. (eds). *Patrick White: A Critical Symposium*. Adelaide: Centre for Research in the New Literatures in English, Flinders University, 1978.

Walsh, William. *Patrick White: 'Voss'*. London: Edward Arnold, 1976.

—— *Patrick White's Fiction*. Sydney: Allen & Unwin, 1977.

Wilkes, G. A. *Ten Essays on Patrick White*. (Selected from *Southerly* (1964–7).) Sydney: Angus & Robertson, 1970.

Selected articles and interviews

Anderson, Don. 'A Severed Leg: Anthropophagy and Communion in Patrick White's Fiction'. *Southerly*, 40 (1980), pp. 399–417.

Brady, Veronica. 'The Eye of the Storm'. *Westerly*, 4 (December 1973), pp. 61–70.

—— 'The Novelist and the New World: Patrick White's *Voss*'. *Texas Studies in Literature and Language*, 21, 2 (Summer 1979), pp. 169–85.

Brissenden, R. F. '*The Vivisector*: Art and Science'. In W. S. Ramson (ed.), *The Australian Experience*, pp. 311–24. Canberra: Australian National University Press, 1974.

Burrows, John. '*Voss* and the Explorers'. *AUMLA*, 26 (November 1966), pp. 234–40.

—— 'The Short Stories of Patrick White'. *Southerly*, 24, 2 (1964) pp. 116–25.

Docker, John. 'Patrick White and Romanticism: *The Vivisector*'. *Southerly*, 33, 1 (March 1973), pp. 44–61.

Green, Dorothy. 'Queen Lear or Cleopatra Rediviva? Patrick White's *The Eye of the Storm*'. *Meanjin Quarterly*, 32 (December 1973), pp. 395–405.

—— '*Voss*: Stubborn Music'. In W. S. Ramson (ed.), *The Australian Experience*, pp. 284–310. Canberra: Australian National University Press, 1974.

Herring, T., and Wilkes, G. A. 'A Conversation with Patrick White'. *Southerly*, 33, 2 (1973), pp. 132–43.

Hetherington, John. 'Patrick White: Life at Castle Hill'. In *Forty Two Faces*, pp. 140–5. Melbourne: Cheshire, 1962.

Kiernan, Brian. 'The Novels of Patrick White'. In Geoffrey Dutton (ed.), *The Literature of Australia*, pp. 461–84. Ringwood, Vic.: Penguin, 1976.

Kramer, Leonie. 'Patrick White: "The Unplayed I"'. *Quadrant*, 18 (February 1974), pp. 65–8.

—— 'Pseudoxia Endemica'. *Quadrant*, 24 (July 1980), pp. 66–7.

Lawson, Alan. 'Unmerciful Dingoes? The Critical Response to Patrick White'. *Meanjin Quarterly*, 32 (December 1973), pp. 379–91.

—— 'Meaning and Experience: A Review-Essay on Some Recurrent Problems in Patrick White Criticism'. *Texas Studies in Literature and Language*, 21, 2 (Summer 1979), pp. 280–95.

Leitch, David. 'Patrick White: A Revealing Profile'. *National Times*, 27 March–1 April 1978, p. 6.

McGregor, Craig. 'Patrick White'. In *In the Making*, pp. 218–22. Melbourne: Nelson, 1969.

Mackenzie, Manfred. '*The Tree of Man*: A Generic Approach'. In John Colmer (ed.), *Approaches to the Novel*, pp. 90–102. Edinburgh: Oliver & Boyd, 1967.

—— 'The Consciousness of "Twin Consciousness": Patrick White's *Solid Mandala*'. *Novel*, 2 (1969), pp. 241–54.

Simons, Margaret. 'Patrick White Finds it Hard To Forgive'. *Age* (Melbourne), 24 September 1983.

Tacey, David. 'A Search for a New Ethic: White's *A Fringe of Leaves*'. In *South Pacific Images* (St Lucia, Qld: South Pacific Association for Commonwealth Language and Literature Studies, 1978), pp. 186–95.

—— 'Denying the Shadow as the Day Lengthens: Patrick White's *The Living and the Dead*'. *Southern Review: An Australian Journal of Literary Studies*, 9 (1978), pp. 165–79.